First published in Great Britain in 1999 by
POETRY NOW YOUNG WRITERS
1-2 Wainman Road, Woodston,
Peterborough, PE2 7BU
Telephone (01733) 230748

All Rights Reserved

Copyright Contributors 1999

HB ISBN 0 75430 281 4
SB ISBN 0 75430 282 2

NORTH HAMPSHIRE

Edited by Carl Golder

FOREWORD

With over 63,000 entries for this year's Cosmic competition, it has proved to be our most demanding editing year to date.

We were, however, helped immensely by the fantastic standard of entries we received, and, on behalf of the Young Writers team, thank you.

The Cosmic series is a tremendous reflection on the writing abilities of 8-11 year old children, and the teachers who have encouraged them must take a great deal of credit.

We hope that you enjoy reading *Cosmic North Hampshire* and that you are impressed with the variety of poems and style with which they are written, giving an insight into the minds of young children and what they think about the world today.

CONTENTS

Jenna Tompkins	35
Hanif Desai	36
Stephanie Critchley	36
Victoria Rossiter	37
Natalie Ramsay	37
Leanne Francis	38
Jamie Marshall	38
Jessica Evans	39
Simon Athawes	40
Alice Turner	41
Woody Martin	41
Melissa Elderfield	42
Helen Thomas	42
Sara Hanna	43
Kerry Wareham	43
Ryan Spinks	44
Maria Lomax	44
Amy White	45
Mark Graham	45
Joseph Sloan	46
Mikaela Buckley	46
Helen McAtamney	47
Paul Moody	47
Elsa Jury	47
Rebecca Collins	48
James Black	48
Samuel Critchley	49
Bradley Hutchins	49
Adam Hunt	49
Jesse James	50
Kayleigh Holt	50
Samantha Theodore	50
William Leadbetter	51
Jamie Lingwood	51
Samantha Ray	52
Sam Hannington	52
Helen Triebel	53
David Fox	53

Robert Leyshon	54
Joely Ball	54
Mark Steggall	55
Kirsty Stewart	55
Adrian Rhoades-Walkley	56
Sarah Branton	56
Paul Fell	57
Guy Grimshawe	57
Thomas Ridley	58
Mark Snell	58
Jonathan Gray	59
Chloe Martin	59
Jessica Skinner	60

Oakley CE Junior School

Amy Keighley	60

Preston Candover CE Primary School

Lucy Harris	61
James Dumelow	61
Christopher Gillman	62
Thomas Cole	62
Rebecca Bennett	63
James Silvester	64
Gemma Cumberlidge	64
Daisy Smith	65
Charlotte Jackson-Stott	65
Peter Wheelwright	66
Tiggy Grafton	66
Frances Swithinbank	67
Sarah Bowden	67
Mark East	68
Ian Simpson	68
Polly Barker	69
Carl Lintott	69
Joanna Travis	70

St Neot's School, Hook

Stephan Randall	70
Andrew MacDonald	71
Katie Reeves	72
Rebecca Harman	72
Lawrence Richards	73
Oliver Hill	73
Giverny Gallagher	74
Steven Dombkouski	74

Tadley Primary School

Nicole Bunn	75
Sophie Bevan	75
Luke Towey	76
Gemma Louise Matthews	76
James Nicholson	77
Micah Bremner	78
Mark Houchin	78
Michelle Tomlinson	79
Katie Mackinnon	80
Richard Nash	80
Joshua Delaney	81
Nick Fletcher	81
Kayleigh Keen	82
Jack Lewis	82
Rebecca Simpson	83
Abby Vincent	83
Abigail King	84
Mereasa Boyes	84
Charlotte Green	85
Bradley Hill	85
Victoria Kyle	85
Kate Turner	86
Chloë Meakes	86
Charlotte Townsend	87
Mark Osborne	87
James Miller	88
Rebecca Hamer	88

Rachael Dolan	89
Ben Bennett	89
Abby-Jade Nicholas	90
Lauren Thompson	90
Iain Lock	91
Katie Lockyer	91
April Bogue	92
Michael Flitter	92
Matthew Jones	93
Danny Nicholas	93
Victoria Wagstaff	94
Kay Goff	94
Mark Fussey	95
Rowan Duncan Arthur	95
Sarah Eaves	96
Calum Douglas	96
Kylie Boyce	97
Chris Boardman	97
Matthew Bunn	98
Katherine Birkinshaw	98
Lucy Boxall	99
Ashley Deller-Merricks	99
Alex Menicou	100

Winklebury Junior School

Joanna Pearce	100
Zakeera Suffee	101
Vincent Bugg	101
Oliver Pullein	102
Sheryl Wild	102
Stephanie Bowles	103
Louise Burt	103
Lauren Austin	104
Jonathan Crook	104
Rachel Harris	105
Vicky Lemm	105
Emma Johnson	106
Mark Frost	106

Worting Junior School

THE POEMS

NEVER STOPS TALKING

She talks in the morning,
She talks at dawn,
She talks on the way to school,
And she talks on the lawn.
She talks in the classroom,
She talks on the stairs,
She talks in assembly,
And when we're saying prayers.
She talks at playtime,
And when we're in PE,
I wish she'd stop the talking,
She's really annoying me!
She talks on the way home,
She talks herself to bed,
That's the end of Bethan Scotford,
She talked till she was dead.

Gemma Fisher (9)
Burnham Copse Junior School

MARS BAR STREET

I live in a very strange place,
not a house, not a bungalow,
but I do live on the moon.
So let's see. You want to know
where I've zoomed all these years.
Well, I've been to Mars Street
and saw an alien made out of choc choc,
which really means chocolate.
But I'm afraid he melted,
        Ahhh!

Abigail Mundy (8)
Burnham Copse Junior School

RUNNING

R unning through the playground
U p and down we go
N ow we're playing it on the lines
N ow we're playing codes.
I n and out playing games
N ow have a rest
G one to kick a ball from the bike shed.

Suzie Robe   (9)
Burnham Copse Junior School

SINGING

She is really good at singing,
I think she's really cool,
Nobody thinks she is sad.
Got to tell everyone how good she is,
I think she should be famous,
Not like the Spice Girls, but like All Saints.
Got to get her *famous!*

Lauren Griffiths (9)
Burnham Copse Junior School

ASTRONAUT

I would like to be an astronaut
So I could fly up in the sky.
Then I could get on the moon.
I could wear a helmet,
Some shoes, and some clothes.
But I would like to go on an aeroplane.

Katrina Occomore (8)
Burnham Copse Junior School

UTTERLY NUTTERLY SPACE

One day I decided to go into space,
I did not know what I was going to face.
I landed on Mars,
Got a few Mars Bars,
And then decided to explore,
And discovered a white floor,
Then realised it was space ice.
I started to slip and slide,
I fell and hurt my backside.
Then I got up,
Saw an alien pup.
He ran off,
I drank some 7-Up,
Realised it was time for bed,
But the aliens would make me dead.
So I went back to Earth,
Where I am now.

Matthew Wright (9)
Burnham Copse Junior School

CRUNCHING

I love crunching, crunching sweets,
But I really hate Shredded Wheats,
I love crunching, crunching crisps
But my favourite crisps are Frisps.

I love crunching, crunching toast,
But I don't like my mum's roast,
I love crunching, crunching food,
But I don't get it, I'm in a mood!

Paula Johnston (10)
Burnham Copse Junior School

EVERYDAY THINGS

When I'm in the playground
I'm always running round like a busy bee.

When I'm crunching chocolate biscuits
I make a mess everywhere.

When I'm bouncing my bouncy ball
it always runs away.

When I'm talking to a friend, my brother's always there
I never get time to talk alone.

When I'm playing with my brother
it's always football.

When I'm skipping round the house
I always break one thing or another.

Liz Pearce (10)
Burnham Copse Junior School

PLAYING IN THE PLAYGROUND

P laying in the playground,
L aughing in the hall,
A ngry in the classroom,
Y oung people laughing in the playground,
G o on, hurry in to class,
R unning on the playground, having fun,
O ut in the playground, children having fun,
U nsupervised children run,
N aughty children go home,
D o not be naughty.

Cathryn Stringer (9)
Burnham Copse Junior School

SPACE TIME

On Monday I made a spaceship,
So on Tuesday I tried it,
and guess what, it did not work.
I tried again on Wednesday,
but it did not work then.
Again and again, I tried once more,
and guess what, it worked at last.
Up and up,
I went so high,
High above the sky I went,
Then it went bang,
I had landed in space.
'Yes,' I shouted,
'I am on the super moon.'

Laura Kite (8)
Burnham Copse Junior School

TALKING

Talking about computers,
Talking about the holidays,
Talking about sweets,
Talking about the weekend,
Talking about cheats,
Talking about games,
Talking about James,

       A
       B
       O
       U
   EveryThing on earth.

Thomas Pearce (10)
Burnham Copse Junior School

BOUNCING

Nicola Brocklehurst is a treat,
She bounces a pea down the street,
She never eats all her tea,
Because she bounces all her peas.

Nicola should be an Olympic bouncer,
And by the way she doesn't weigh ounces,
Nicola bounces her pea across the floor,
And then she asks her mum for more.

She bounces at the seaside,
She bounces thin and wide,
Nicola bounces on the car,
Nicola bounces a bit too far.

At the end of the day,
Nicola is not far away,
She is in her bedroom,
Staring at the moon.

Her mum comes in and puts her to bed,
Nicola Brocklehurst bounces on her head,
Then the next morning,
She is bouncing and her mum is yawning.

Bethan Scotford (10)
Burnham Copse Junior School

RUNNING

Hot, sweating, panting,
Running from your friends,
In and out.

Charlotte Simmonds (9)
Burnham Copse Junior School

PLAYGROUND FUN

P laying in the playground, skipping by the wall
L ay down your skipping rope and go in the hall
A fight in the playground brings people running
Y oung children shouting for the fight to go on
G o on the playground, pick it up again
R un around the playground being chased in
O utside in the playground bell goes again, start work again
U nderneath the table, oh no, I've been found out
N ow I have to miss my play
D own by the staff

F ull with work to do
U nless I cheat?
N o I'd better not. Oh well, that's the end of me.

Abigail Lewis (9)
Burnham Copse Junior School

JUMPING IN THE PLAYGROUND .

Jumping high
Whizzing past
Up in the air
Everyone stare
Slowly, fast, then at last
Then a crash
And a dash
All the way to the hospital
I was out in a dash, everyone looked at me
So I stopped jumping and
went home for tea.

Jon Geering (9)
Burnham Copse Junior School

NUTSY IN SPACE

I once saw a spaceship high above the sky,
In that spaceship I saw
Crabs, they saw the captain come in,
The crabs went to battle stations,
'Crab attack' said one,
All the crabs got killed,
Nutsy the crab was still alive,
He crashed . . . *bang,*
Nutsy got out of the spaceship,
'I name this planet Nutsy,'
But just then he saw a flag
'Alien Earth' it said
And the aliens killed him.
There was an earthquake,
And all the aliens died.

Nicholas Stewart (8)
Burnham Copse Junior School

THE FOOTBALL MATCH

It's my first ever football match for the school team.
I can't wait till it's half-time.
Cos then it's ice-cream.
And I hope I don't get sent off cos it's a crime.

I'm very nervous for my first match.
I'm in defence, what if I lose the ball?
I hope the keeper makes a good catch.
If I want the ball I'd better call.

Jamie Allen (9)
Burnham Copse Junior School

I LOVE DANCING

I love dancing, dancing in the street.
I love dancing in the heat.
I love dancing, dancing in the sea.
I love dancing everywhere.
Even in my bed.
Even when I'm dead.
>   *And it never ends.*

Danielle Bridge (10)
Burnham Copse Junior School

I LOVE TALKING

I love talking, talking about food.
I love talking about you.
I love talking in the swimming pool.
I love talking in the school.
I love talking in my bed.
I love talking till I'm dead.

Cheryl Pope (9)
Burnham Copse Junior School

WHIZZING ROCKETS

Shooting,
In the night sky,
Rockets go whizzing by.
Rockets are landing on Pluto,
See you.

Sarah Pulley (9)
Burnham Copse Junior School

INTERGALACTIC SPACEMAN

I want to be an
intergalactic spaceman,
So I can see what's
up there.
So I can see
the monsters.
So I can float
in space.
And I went
to a galaxy.
And then
I went back again.
I went to Mars
to stick a bar
in the ground.
I met Julian Golly
who plays baseball
in space.
Did I tell you that
I went on a
supersonic spoon
to space?

Simon McCarthy (7)
Burnham Copse Junior School

TALKING

Words came from my mouth
noisy and very loudly
talking everywhere.

Carol Endean (9)
Burnham Copse Junior School

THE MILKY WAY

My mum gave me a toy rocket
But I wanted a very real rocket
But she won't get me one
Because it would be too much fun.
But I will make one of my own
Made of metal round the dome.
So I said 'By the way
I'm going to the Milky Way.'
Through the roof, and up in space
See all the planets that I face.
Look, the Moon
I'll be there soon.
Wow, let's get a cup of tea
But when I zoomed home I had a flea.
So mum said 'Filthy boy
Go in the bath and play with a toy.'

Darren Mawson (9)
Burnham Copse Junior School

MY TEACHER WENT UP TO SPACE

My teacher went up to space with a zoom.
She saw a planet called Mars.
She saw a goblin.
She took a pair of flying shoes
          and
          flew
          back
          home.

Emma Francis (8)
Burnham Copse Junior School

ALIEN EYES

I wish I was an alien,
They live on planet Mars,
They have bulging black eyes,
Their faces are grey,
I would like to have hands like them,
I wish I was an alien, but then again,
We are people.

Kerry Hoblyn (9)
Burnham Copse Junior School

THE GREY PIZZA

I had a grey pizza,
That flew through my mum's bedroom
And went into my spaceship.
I whacked it right into space,
Raced on a planet,
So go to space.

Matthew Cox (9)
Burnham Copse Junior School

I WANTED TO GO TO MARS

I wanted to go to Mars,
To pass the shining star,
I looked in my pocket,
And picked out a rocket,
And shot myself off to Mars.

Hayley Collard (8)
Burnham Copse Junior School

COMET

Comet whizzing in the night,
Shining bright,
Hardly seen, normally out of sight.
It's so hard to see, it's more like a blur of light,
Probably because it's as fast as light.
It travels from star to star,
By day or night,
It's a very extraordinary sight.
Normally seen by telescope with long sight,
This comet I know well,
It's called Haley's comet.
It comes and goes every 76 years.
You might see it if you've got long eyesight.

Robert Read (9)
Burnham Copse Junior School

MARS

In the night
I saw a planet.
I thought it
Was the Moon.
But then I thought,
Oh no, it's Mars.
Yes, I saw!
It's Mars I saw!
Up in the sky with stars
I saw the Milky Way
Shining far away.

Rhys Jones (8)
Burnham Copse Junior School

ALIENS IN SPACE

Aliens in space,
Show their ugly face,
They have four eyes,
And eat stinky pies,
They probably have spiky hairstyles,
And secret files,
Pointy and chubby noses,
Letting their horrible pets eat roses.

Daniel Lowe (8)
Burnham Copse Junior School

THE BIG ROCKET

There was a big rocket,
Zoom up into space,
It goes to Mars, Pluto, Saturn,
And back to the Earth.
Rockets squirt fire out the back,
Rockets, rockets.

Laura Bolland (8)
Burnham Copse Junior School

TAZ ESCAPES FROM MARS

Taz went to Mars, and got caught by stars,
He moaned and he groaned, but they've never let him go.
He said 'Hooray' in the year 2001,
He hopped in a ship, he said 'Bye Mars.'

Terry Fuller (9)
Burnham Copse Junior School

MY ALIEN MATE FROM OUTER SPACE

My alien mate from outer space,
Came down to my house one day.
Never know what he did, he ate and ate and ate,
Never know what he was eating, it was a mouse in my house.
But the strangest thing was,
It came from planet Coz.
I wish I was an alien that goes around Mars
or Jupiter or the Moon.
I'll just wait a while,
Because my turn will come soon.
I asked my mum, she said don't be silly,
I asked my dad who was telling off Billy.
So I went to space to alien town,
And here I am wearing a beautiful crown.

Richard Marwood (9)
Burnham Copse Junior School

THE GREATEST ADVENTURE OF THE SKY

Space, space, I'm high in space,
And I'm flying in space.
Just then I landed on a planet,
And I saw Mars from the planet I was on,
And out popped an alien and I was scared to death.
I fell off the planet,
I landed on the Earth.
I was very upset,
I missed the alien very much.

Katie Scriven (8)
Burnham Copse Junior School

MY COUSIN

My cousin,
He never thinks first,
For example,
Take a day last week,
He wanted a trip into space,
When all of a sudden,
There was an explosion,
And he zoomed out
Through the roof,
He then caught a spaceship,
And went on a trip
To Jupiter, Venus and Mars,
He then caught a flying saucer,
Flown by slimy aliens,
Through the blazing
Stars and comets.

Clare Hallcup (9)
Burnham Copse Junior School

MY SPACE ADVENTURE

I am,
In a rocket,
Going up to the stars,
Landed on the moon, met a spoon,
Went back home,
To see my mum
And told her I saw the sun,
My mum did not believe me,
Maybe I just imagined it!

Claire Dyson (8)
Burnham Copse Junior School

TRAVELLING INTO SPACE

Space, space,
I travelled up into the sky
But very very high,
A great rocket came flying by,
It was dark and I was frightened.
I was very very cold,
I was flying up and down,
And fell down to Mars.
Some aliens popped out,
And scared me out of my skin.
My rocket had broken,
I was scared stiff, still,
I stayed there for five weeks.
I was sad and lonely,
Bored to tears too,
But then I thought
I'm not alone, I'm with the aliens,
And I fell down to Earth,
And I crashed.
I forgot all about it then.

Samantha Turner (8)
Burnham Copse Junior School

MY COUSIN

My cousin said the moon had a man inside,
And he wishes to go and see him.
My Aunty Margaret bought a spaceship for him,
And the spaceship got there at last.

Mary Wall (8)
Burnham Copse Junior School

SPACE HOCKEY

Flying in my space car to the mystic star,
We've gone so far,
Just to see the magic match,
We've undone the car latch,
Going to the mystic match,
Mighty aliens v Saturn aliens,
Who knows who is going to win,
From Pluto to Uranus to Mars,
All kinds of aliens are coming to the hockey match,
The referee drops the star puck,
Mighty aliens with the star puck,
Goal,
Mighty aliens *win!*

Joel Green (8)
Burnham Copse Junior School

THE MILKY WAY

I went to the Milky Way in a rocket,
And on the way there, I saw a galaxy.
Later I saw the planet Sun.
A little bit further on I saw lots of aliens
Dancing around some stars.
Then I said to myself 'They are insane'
And went on.
Soon after I saw an alien funfair,
Then shouted *'Ahhh'*
And flew home.

Roseanne Kelly (8)
Burnham Copse Junior School

WHAT IS SPACE LIKE?

'Brother, brother
What is space like?
Is it like
Taking a hike?'
I said 'No way,
Maybe I'll tell you
Another day.'
Then next day
Guess what he said!
'What is . . . '
'Shut up or . . .
I'll knock off your head.'
Then next day
He just got strict
Cos people were picking on him.
'Okay - space is not down below
It's up in the air - we all know.'
Is that fair?
Look at all the shiny stars
Look! Just see Mars.

Lewis Dyment (9)
Burnham Copse Junior School

I'M WHIZZING THROUGH SPACE

I'm whizzing through space,
In my new spaceship,
Past the Moon and the stars,
I'm off to Mars, then I can see
The Moon soon.

Alex Southgate (9)
Burnham Copse Junior School

MY PETS

My cat Sophie is very fluffy.
I have a dog, her name is Muffy.
Angelica's not very old,
Her body's white, her head is gold.

Sophie's a scritchy, scratchy cat.
She bites just like a vampire bat.
Muff, poor dog, she's old but sweet,
And loves it when she gets a treat.

My angel fish is tropical,
She's rather large, she isn't small.
I love my pets, they are the best,
They are better than the rest!

Morag Hamilton (11)
Burnham Copse Junior School

THE MOON

I travelled to the Moon,
In a blazing rocket,
I ate this special food,
And then I landed,
On the Moon,
I had a drink,
I'll be back soon,
I got to Earth,
We had to work,
Home at last.

James Hobbs (9)
Burnham Copse Junior School

SPACE ATTACK

There once was an alien.
This alien has eight million eyes.
The alien had an attack and
Then broke his back
But then he saw me.
The alien chased me all around the earth.
He set his tongue and broke his brain
I triple-jumped to the moon
And he tried to jump to the moon.
He got there before me.
Just as I got there
He tried to smack me in the face
But I gave him a smack in the face
And knocked him out.
He opened his eyes
And saw me jump back to earth.
No you bit my back.

James Scanlan (7)
Burnham Copse Junior School

MY SPACE HOLIDAY

I went to the Moon in a rocket,
Whizz! Zoom!
Here I come,
Bye, mum!
I go past Mars,
I won't miss my class,
I will not give my mum
A fright at night,
Bye!

Christopher Smeeth (8)
Burnham Copse Junior School

SPACE JUMP

I jumped
to the Moon
then I jumped
to planet Pluto
then I jumped
back down to Earth.

Then my sister
jumped onto the Moon
then she jumped
to planet Pluto
then she jumped
back down to Earth.

Thomas Harris (8)
Burnham Copse Junior School

I BUILT A SPACESHIP

I built a spaceship
But my brother said
It was a racing ship
So I went inside
Took off and went to Uranus
I planted some seeds but they
Shot up in the air
And burned on the Sun
So I got on my space hopper
And hopped to Mars
I said 'I don't like it here'
So I zoomed back to Earth.

Liam Jones (8)
Burnham Copse Junior School

GYMNASTICS

Gymnastics.
Gymnastics is great,
A sport that's fun,
Mrs Woods is the best,
Better than all the rest.
Gymnastics.
We jump the boxes,
Climb the ropes,
We practise our rolls,
Forward and backward rolls.
Gymnastics.
We love to leapfrog,
Practise our straddle,
On Tuesday mornings,
Tuesday evenings.
Gymnastics.
Nicola, Jo, Toni,
Morag can clear the box,
We try our best,
But can't beat the rest.
Gymnastics.

Joanne Gemmell (10)
Burnham Copse Junior School

ROCKET

Rocket
Lands on the Moon
Lands on different planets
Oh rocket down the Milky Way
Rocket.

Joanne Bratt (8)
Burnham Copse Junior School

MY CAT

My cat,
His piercing green eyes,
Always stare at you,
My cat,
His felty nose always twitching,
At the slightest sound.

My cat,
His glimmering whiskers,
Shining in the sun,
My cat,
His velvety ears,
Love being stroked.

My cat,
His sharp claws,
Are sharpened every day,
My cat,
His long black tail,
Swinging when he's excited.

Kristy Steggall (11)
Burnham Copse Junior School

SPACE ATTACK

Once upon a time
A little boy wanted to go to the moon,
And his mum said yes,
So he went and got ready.
He brought a big spoon and a big yoghurt.
So he went to the moon and when he got there
He saw a monster who scared the little boy away.

Nicole Hoblyn (7)
Burnham Copse Junior School

BODYBOARDING

Bodyboarding,
Walking slowly
Through the harsh coldness of the sea.
Sand tickles in my wetsuit
Finding a place to stop.

Bodyboarding,
1, 2, 3, and away I go,
Whizzing towards the shore,
Salty waves crashing over my head.
Coming to a jerky stop.

Bodyboarding,
Tall, towering waves
Rushing towards me,
Falling off, waves enclosing over my head.
Time to go home now - but it was fun!

Catherine Read (10)
Burnham Copse Junior School

MARS ATTACK

They were coming down, down.
They were coming down.
That is if they won't come down.
I won't just stand there.
Well go on then.
But you have not got time.
But if you got there.
Well what are you waiting for?

Mars is attacking.

Jack Wishart (8)
Burnham Copse Junior School

KARATE CAPERS

Welcome to the world of war,
Where punishment settles the score.
I'll try to tell you all my friends,
From beginning to end.

First the kicking,
That's where the teachers like picking,
Then there's blocks
As the gymnasium clock tocks.
Belts red, yellow, black and blue,
And in the end you'll be the colour of the last two.

Goodbye my friend,
I must go, karate about to start.

Genevieve Ray (10)
Burnham Copse Junior School

MY DOPEY DOG

My dopey dog
is a very dopey dog.
I sometimes wonder
what she is doing.
She really is a dopey dog.

My dopey owner
is a very dopey owner.
I sometimes wonder
why he has his nostrils
in a newspaper.
My dopey owner
is a very dopey owner.

Stefan Triebel (11)
Burnham Copse Junior School

I Love My Hamsters

Sniffle, sniffle, rustle, rustle,
My hamsters have woken up to play.
Sniffle, sniffle, rustle, rustle,
'Come on Twix, come on Spot,' is what I say.

Munch, munch, nibble, nibble,
My hamsters are eating a sunflower seed.
Munch, munch, nibble, nibble,
A drink is next that they need.

Scratch, scratch, itch, itch,
My hamsters are cleaning themselves quite fast.
Scratch, scratch, itch, itch,
And they're going to bed at last.

Kirstie Broadhead (11)
Burnham Copse Junior School

Grandpa

Grandpa sits upon his chair,
And on his head he has some hair.
The hair is grey,
But that's OK,
'Cause we still love him anyway.

Then Grandpa died,
And we all cried,
And we all said 'Bye, bye.'

Shem Bartley (11)
Burnham Copse Junior School

SWIMMING

I go down to the swimming pool,
To get myself cool.
I splash, splish and splosh,
I swim, dive and race my friend.

Fun never ends,
She always beats me,
But it doesn't bother me.
That's because we're friends.

We stay all day,
Then shout *hooray!*
It's a Saturday
Then we go there again.

Kate Munday (11)
Burnham Copse Junior School

SPORTS CARS

Ferrari, Aston Martin, BMW, Jaguar,
McLaren, Dodge Viper, Lotus and Volvo
What a complete selection.

The suspension, the 0-60, the 60-0
V12 engines, V10 engines
My, these cars really must fly.

Seven gears if automatic, five gears if not.
The steering, the ABS,
All sports cars will have some of these.

> *But we guarantee they go*
> *like the wind.*

Mark King (10)
Burnham Copse Junior School

FORMULA ONE

Williams, Benetton, McLaren and Ferrari
All finished in the top ten.
What a finale.
Villeneuve's in the pits, Schumacher goes through,
Here's Panis and he's spun and his engine's gone.

Eddie Irvine finished first
Ten seconds later, Michael,
Mica Hakkinen came in third
With Coulthard close behind.

The Constructors' Champion went to Ferrari,
The drivers' went to Irvine
Schumacher got second place,
With Damon Hill in third.

Tom Ensom (11)
Burnham Copse Junior School

BASKETBALL

B ouncing the basketball.
A ttempting to get the basketball.
S hooting at the basket.
K nocking the ball out the opponent's hands.
E arly in the game a player went off.
T rying as hard as we can.
B asketball is fun.
A ltogether now.
L et us win.
L et's win!

Marc Young (11)
Burnham Copse Junior School

BUG WAR

Slugs versus the Cockroaches,
There's gonna be a war,
Big Fred, the snail, the referee.
He's gonna hold the score.

> There's lots of squishing.
> Black squidge everywhere.
> Centipedes, Parasites,
> Dung beetles. Beware!

There's been lots of squishing and squashing
But now the end's come.
The Slugs still have ten slugs left
The Cockroaches have none!

Lauren Rhoades-Walkley (10)
Burnham Copse Junior School

SPACE

Silent and dark planets are glowing,
In space, gloomy and quiet.
Out of the window you can see
Shooting stars, comets and darkness.

Never-ending gloominess shines in the dark,
Yellows and reds, oranges,
Dusty and lonely, dark and peaceful,
See the comets whiz by.

Warm and dark in the rocket,
Whizzing past the planets,
Catch the stars as we go past,
Home we go to Earth below.

Kirsty Duggan (9)
Burnham Copse Junior School

RUNNING

Running is my favourite sport,
I wear my new trainers,
With my T-shirt and shorts.
With my instructor I learn to run faster.
Running is my favourite sport.

Running down the track,
He encourages me to get to the finish,
The gun goes and we're off,
We have to go round the track three times,
The finish is near.

We had passed the finish and I came first,
My dad gave me confidence.
I thanked my instructor,
He thanked me,
And we all burst out with glee.

Some nights it's raining,
Whatever the weather,
I go running,
With my instructor,
Rain or sunshine.

Nicola Simmonds (11)
Burnham Copse Junior School

COSMIC

Flying saucers through the sky
Seeing comets as they fly
Shooting stars flying by before
My eyes in the sky.

Stephanie Martinez-Garcia (9)
Burnham Copse Junior School

SPACE IS A WONDERFUL PLACE

Space is a wonderful place
So big, so wide
Lots of space
Dark and gloomy, stars everywhere.

Space is a wonderful place for aliens
Green and slimy, fat and small,
Big fat pimples on them all.

Space is a wonderful place,
Shooting stars, planets, comets
Space is a wonderful place for all.

Gemma Smith (10)
Burnham Copse Junior School

UP IN SPACE

We are in space,
It's dark up here,
It's spooky up here too,
It's quiet.

Look at those shiny stars,
There's an enormous moon,
The stars are shooting,
And we're going round and round.

Ahhhh! I can't see,
We have landed on Mars
Or Jupiter, what can it be?
We're stranded here forever.

Lynn Richardson (11)
Burnham Copse Junior School

THE ALIEN WHO WANTED TO FLY

A long time ago
On the planet Pluto
An alien wanted to fly
High up in the sky.

He got into space
He was a spaceship ace
Who sent away for a pizza
The toppings were gunge and fizza.

He landed on his planet
And met Zig the bandit
He saw his mum and dad
Just imagine the fun he had!

Gary Roberts (11)
Burnham Copse Junior School

CAPTAIN PICARD

Zig, zag, zoom!
The exhaust went boom
An alien came by
And saw the USS Enterprise.

Data said 'Oh look, my brother'
John Luke said, 'Oh, don't bother
He's just a stupid alien
There's no room for Martian men.'

Oh dong it
You space Cadet
I really really want to whiz
In fact I'll have a cola fizz.

Carlie Wishart (10)
Burnham Copse Junior School

BLAST-OFF

Up in the shuttle,
Ready to lift off,
Countdown has started,
4, 3, 2, 1, *blast-off!*

In the blackness up they go,
Shuttle splitting in half,
In and out around the planets,
The stars are light tonight.

We're losing control,
We're going down, down, down,
We've landed on Jupiter,
Will be here forever.

Laura Spickett (11)
Burnham Copse Junior School

SPACE POEM

The atmosphere is gloomy and dark
Shooting stars leaving sparks.
Comets are flying through the air,
No gravity, it's hot and bare.

The Earth twisting round and round
UFOs dare not touch the ground.
Rockets are zooming through the stars,
Slimy aliens asleep on Mars.

Little flowers appearing on the moon,
I should be leaving very soon.
Thank you for listening to me.
See you soon as can be.

Fiona Allan (10)
Burnham Copse Junior School

THE TRIP INTO SPACE

Stars, stars, lots of stars,
Shining in the sky,
The moon and lots of planets,
Whiz past me as I fly.

The rocket circles around the world,
Little dots are what I see,
But really they are mountains,
Rivers, and the sea.

I don't know where I'm going,
Or where I'm going to be,
But hopefully, it's back to Earth,
And not be late for tea!

Jessica Sayers (11)
Burnham Copse Junior School

THE TRAVEL

5, 4, 3, 2, 1, blast-off!
Up, up and away
Say goodbye to ground
And hello to the sky.

As you travel on and on
In this never-ending sky
See a shooting star fly past
And the big planets.

See the sun so big
And then see the moon
Now it's time to say goodbye
Whizzing back to land.

Jenna Tompkins (11)
Burnham Copse Junior School

SPACE - AN EMPTY PLACE TO BE

When I first see space
It's an empty place,
Dark and bright wherever you are,
But no aliens so far.

All I see is twinkly stars,
Until I see planet Mars
Mars is huge but also boring,
Because no aliens are really snoring.

Now I leave Mars,
There's still lots of stars,
The description of space to me,
Is an empty place to be.

Hanif Desai (11)
Burnham Copse Junior School

COSMIC!

Shooting rocket;
Zooming off to space.
Orbiting the moon;
Crashing there.
Watch the comet flickering on its way past
I wonder where it's going?
Shining, silvery moon;
Shimmering stars;
Mars the red;
Many other planets too.
I wonder what else is up there?

Stephanie Critchley (10)
Burnham Copse Junior School

MARS!

I'm the first man on Mars,
a terrible place.
I come from the stars
it's a wonderful place in space.
But here on Mars
I think I shall pass,
I don't like it here at all.

It's all red and bright.
Big and light.
Look at the shadowy places,
And all those horrible faces.
I'm not going to stay.
I'm running away
From this horrible, scary place.

Victoria Rossiter (9)
Burnham Copse Junior School

COSMIC

My dad's an astronaut.
He tells me
that the galaxy is
much too big for me.
The Milky Way is
many light years away.
The stars are so white,
especially bright.

I'm glad my dad's an astronaut.

Natalie Ramsay (10)
Burnham Copse Junior School

COSMIC

The space shuttle's ready,
You're not very steady,
The countdown is on,
10, 9, 8, 7, 6, 5, 4, 3, 2, 1, 0 . . .
And you're gone.
You feel like a hero,
You look at the stars,
And fly past Mars.
You zoom to the moon,
I hope you will come home soon.
You see asteroids and the supernova.
I would fly to Saturn.
Off we go,
Me and Co,
It's time to say goodbye.

Goodbye!

Leanne Francis (11)
Burnham Copse Junior School

COSMIC!

L ost in space without a hope.
I   n the distance is a blurred shape
G oing at light speed,
H eading towards us.
T railing behind are another few hundred.
S creams are heard from
P etrified people.
E very second
E dging nearer
D anger is here, we all know that!

Jamie Marshall (10)
Burnham Copse Junior School

COSMIC!

The shuttle's about to go
you're ready
the countdown starts
and you're steady
but wait . . .
you stop
can I get off?
Surely I don't have to go?
5 . . .
just think of all the asteroids
zooming up and down
round and round and round
and what about those aliens
I just can't resist?
Surely they don't exist
4 . . .
the black holes, the Milky Way
the satellites, I start to say
3 . . .
Mars and Venus will I see them?
The lovely moon I wonder when
2 . . .
but what about the moon buggy?
I don't have a driving licence.
1 . . .

The shooting stars, the Co . . .
at 13.27 hrs the shuttle Guinevere has left our atmosphere
let's hope they have a pleasant journey.

Jessica Evans (10)
Burnham Copse Junior School

COSMIC!

Uranus, Jupiter, Mars and Saturn,
The solar system is a pattern;
Pluto, Mercury and Neptune,
The planets are bigger than giant balloons!
Comets, stars and asteroids,
But I haven't seen a droid.
Aliens and alien ships,
No! They don't eat fish and chips!
Monsters' grime,
And serpents' slime:
Rocket ship lasers,
Don't fly over quasers!
Flying saucers and man-eating things,
Creatures with spikes and some with wings:
Bazookas, Uzis and a shotgun,
Guns can be a bit of fun!
The aliens are back,
They've come back to attack:
Surrounding me,
With beams of energy!
Bang!
What's this? I'm still alive!
Alright! Now give me five:
I thought I needed first aid,
But I'm only at the arcade!

Simon Athawes (9)
Burnham Copse Junior School

SHE TALKS

She talks at the table,
She talks in the stable.
She talks to her cat,
She talks when she's putting on her hat.

She talks to her dad,
Her dad thinks she's mad.
She talks when she's making a cake,
She talks in the woods down by the lake.

She talks in art,
She talks in the hall when we're eating treacle tart.
She talks at the shops,
She talks in class when we're counting bottle tops.

She talks when she has a snack of fruit,
She talks when she's cleaning her brother's football boots.
She talks when she's out spending money,
She talks when eating toast with honey.

Alice Turner (10)
Burnham Copse Junior School

COSMIC!

A liens in the Cosmos
L anding on Mars, Jupiter and Earth
I   n a flying saucer
E ven as we speak they're conquering
N eptune and Saturn
S pace, a big open place!

Woody Martin (9)
Burnham Copse Junior School

COSMIC

Cosmic space
is such a big place,
green monsters that look like slime,
riding in spaceships fast and fine,
astronauts that come from the UK,
looking around the Milky Way,
comets flying in a race,
knocking astronauts out of their place,
black holes sucking everything up,
everything that's sucked up is eaten as tuck,
up in space it's such a wonderful place,
it's boring down here . . .
Space is where I want to be!

Melissa Elderfield (9)
Burnham Copse Junior School

COSMIC

I was lying on my back
Looking up to the sky
Shooting stars fly by before my eye.
This is the year for the comet to pass,
Right over the Earth while I am watching.
I caught a glimpse of something light and bright
A spaceship?
I called my friend to have a look,
Before she arrived
It had melted away
Did I imagine it all?

Helen Thomas (10)
Burnham Copse Junior School

SPACE LIFE

If I was a spaceman
I would fly to Zogodar to jump on a trampoline
I would go too far
If I was a spaceman I would go to Sooz
(which in other words is 'zoos').
I would learn the alien alphabet AEU
No teacher would fly two miles to say 'Boo!'
I would find a living zebra and a kangaroo
I would jump to Jupiter and Mars too
I'd climb space trees
To pick purple food
I would eat sun sweets
Pink potatoes too.
The alien washed all the windows, doors, too
Alien ideas would go round my head
Inside, outside, and round instead.

Sara Hanna (8)
Burnham Copse Junior School

COSMIC

Stars just sitting here and there
Comets zooming everywhere
A spaceship is having a battle
With a local UFO
Another ship is heading straight for the moon
They're nearly there
About an hour or two, or even three
I wonder if they'll be there by tea.

Kerry Wareham (9)
Burnham Copse Junior School

SPACE BALL

I kicked a ball and
out it went to space
to space. A week later I wondered
where it went, so . . . I kicked myself to
space, to space. *Wwweeeee*. I go off to space
to space, I went to the Milky Way
to play footie for a day, a day.
I went to Jupiter. I played on
the computer. I went to
Mars and played with
my toy cars. But still
no ball, no ball.
I went to the
moon
and found a spoon but still
no ball. But then
I thought
I may not
find it
at all.

Ryan Spinks (8)
Burnham Copse Junior School

COSMIC

Shooting stars whizzing by
Flying saucers everywhere!
Rockets flying up in the sky
Stars so bright they hurt my eyes.
Aliens are landing, *watch out!*

Maria Lomax (10)
Burnham Copse Junior School

I GO TO SPACE

I'm a silly astronaut,
I went to space,
I met an alien with a funny face,
His eyes were no bigger
than a toy car race,
His neck was as long as a giraffe's face,
His belly was the same shape as a telly,
He lives in a pig sty and his name is Kai,
Look, look
over there a family sitting in an armchair,
They are bright pink with black spots
and the baby has the chickenpox,
Oh no it's time to go
one hour gone
so long.

Amy White (8)
Burnham Copse Junior School

SPACESHIP

One day I saw a spaceship,
Land in my bedroom.
Then I saw a yellow light peeking out from the bottom.
It took me to space and played ice hockey
On a planet called Iceland from town centre,
And a shop called Forbuoys and one more shop
Called 'If you are thirsty'.
So Max said 'Let's get a drink,' and took me
back for tea.

Mark Graham (8)
Burnham Copse Junior School

SPACE

Space is wacky,
Space is great,
Space looks like something my little sister ate!
I went to school the next day,
We went to Mars with no delay,
On a big spaceship with my sister,
There was a fat boy at the front,
He was too fat and plump,
He can't go!
We all yelled,
So he didn't,
He stayed at home,
Good job too,
He wouldn't fit in!

Joseph Sloan (8)
Burnham Copse Junior School

THE BOUNCY ALIEN

Once I saw an alien trying to bounce to
the zoo.
So I took him to the kangaroos and
they bounced with
him too.
But then he met a wallaby and it had
thick blue skin
and wouldn't you
be surprised, it bounced with
him too.

Mikaela Buckley (7)
Burnham Copse Junior School

MARS BARS

I am an astronaut
And I am going to Mars
I'm not going to take any food with me
Because I am going to Mars
And on Mars the only
Thing you eat is Mars Bars
So let's get on with it
Ten, nine, eight, seven, six
Five, four, three, two, one
Off we go to *space!*

Helen McAtamney (7)
Burnham Copse Junior School

SPACE ZAXON

I went to the Moon, I went to the stars
In a spaceship I went to Space Zaxon
I met an alien, I hit him by mistake
I took him home, he woke up and went to Zaxon.
I always visit him on Zaxon Day.

Paul Moody (8)
Burnham Copse Junior School

SPACE

Simon went to the moon.
Panda bear went to the moon as well at 10 o'clock.
They came home at 1 o'clock to eat their lunch.

Elsa Jury (8)
Burnham Copse Junior School

PANCAKE DAY

On Pancake Day my friends,
Mummy saw an old man
From the moon.
His laugh was awful
But as soon as he whistled
Something came up.
In a flash he said that
It must be my flying saucer
Whooshing to me
But it was not a flying saucer
It was a pancake.

Rebecca Collins (8)
Burnham Copse Junior School

SPACE

A flying saucer
A spaceship
And an alien and
a human
And I saw them too

I screamed!

And everyone heard me
So they said 'Shut up!
So I read.

James Black (8)
Burnham Copse Junior School

SPACE WORLD

Aliens.
Aliens live in space
live in rockets.
Ten, nine, eight, seven, six.
Rockets went right up to space
and don't forget aliens.
Aliens are different to you.
Aliens have four eyes
to see all of space.

Samuel Critchley (8)
Burnham Copse Junior School

WHEN I WENT TO SPACE

I went to space,
I jumped on the moon.
Then I saw an alien,
I said 'What's your hobby?'
'I have not got one.'
I said 'Well I have.
Mine is coming to space every day.'

Bradley Hutchins (8)
Burnham Copse Junior School

UFOS

I saw a shining light, at first I thought it was an aeroplane.
Shining bright, it landed in the bushes and I had fright.
I saw one little alien called Freddie, he became my friend.

Adam Hunt (9)
Burnham Copse Junior School

SUPERSTAR

Knock, knock.
Who's there?
Aliens from space.
What do you want alien?
I want to eat you.
No you're not because I'm an alien too
and I'm going to eat *you!*

Jesse James (8)
Burnham Copse Junior School

THE MONSTER IN SPACE WITH THE CAT

There was a monster in space
I hated his face, he lived in a spaceship
And it looked like a face ship
Then I met this cat, she was a little rat
Then a spaceship killed her and
That was the end of the cat.

Kayleigh Holt (8)
Burnham Copse Junior School

SPACE

There is a strange place called space,
It hit my brother in the face.
He found a rocket, it didn't work,
He said whoever made this is a jerk.
He went back down to earth one day,
The next morning he said 'Hooray.'

Samantha Theodore (7)
Burnham Copse Junior School

SPACE TROUBLE

I travelled far up into space and
saw a super flying machine.
I said 'Cool who's in there?'
and all I heard
was a big *bang* and
again I said 'Who's in there?'
and it was my cousin Mickey,
but then we heard a
massive *bang*
and there was an alien
but then I heard a
peculiar voice.
The alien
said 'Don't be afraid, it's
me dad!'

William Leadbetter (8)
Burnham Copse Junior School

COMETS

Shooting comets in the sky
I don't know how fast they fly
But did you ever, ever wonder
What happens to the lightning and thunder?
Does it still go crackling
Through the sky or does
It just blow up and simply die?

Jamie Lingwood (9)
Burnham Copse Junior School

A DREAM

I had a dream,
It felt like cream,
I married an alien,
He was in disguise,
And gave me a surprise,
He gave me a ring,
Which made a ting,
He was called Sim,
His surname Tim,
I thought if I had a baby,
It would be very fabby,
Then I woke up,
And had a cup of tea.

Samantha Ray (8)
Burnham Copse Junior School

THE MOON

On the moon spacemen going to the moon in spaceships,
they may be finding monsters and aliens about to attack the sun
but I think they will get frazzled up.
But one day they might start attacking us,
ready with rifles, and machine guns.
Get ready to fight but you do not know
one day it might happen.

Sam Hannington (9)
Burnham Copse Junior School

STARS STARS

Shining bright
twinkling in
the night
the Great Bear
the Plough
the Dog
to name a
few
they are
all looking
down on
you.

Helen Triebel (7)
Burnham Copse Junior School

SPACE TIME

Golden stars
Silver moon
Golden Milky Way
Cold ice
Bright sun
Shining flying saucers
Creepy aliens
Flaming sun.

David Fox (7)
Burnham Copse Junior School

THE SPACEMAN

I went up into space
I saw a funny face
It wasn't a human
It wasn't an animal
It must have been an alien from outer space
It came up to me
It liked to lick its knee
But I wasn't frightened
Because I found out he was my friend
Because he was meant to guide me to Mars
And I got lots of chocolate bars
And when that was over I went home to my space shuttle.

Robert Leyshon (7)
Burnham Copse Junior School

ASTRONAUTS

Astronauts are tall,
Astronauts are small,
Astronauts are high,
In the sky,
Zooming around,
To the ground,
Up again,
They're insane!

Joely Ball (7)
Burnham Copse Junior School

Up In Space

Flying saucers
Stars, galaxy
Planets weightless
Milky Way flaming
Moon airless
Mars cold
Rocky Saturn
Pluto hard
Sun hot
Space dark
Astronauts cold
Alien creepy.

Mark Steggall (7)
Burnham Copse Junior School

Mars

I would like to go to Mars,
Look down on the million stars.
I am an astronaut,
I flew right from the airport.
I had a picnic on the moon
And bought a bright pink balloon.
I was still in space,
But could not go at a very fast pace!

Kirsty Stewart (8)
Burnham Copse Junior School

UFO

I saw a UFO in the dark night, then a few seconds later
I saw a shiny light
There were aliens all around me
Even underground they tried to trap me
I tried to run away but the aliens covered me up
With a cage!
They tried to shoot me with a laser, I dodged the lasers
And I crawled through the cage.
I ran away and I was lucky not to stay there.
If you see a UFO just walk off and go
Don't stay there otherwise you'll get shot by a laser.

Adrian Rhoades-Walkley (9)
Burnham Copse Junior School

SPACE

The stars are
in space and
rockets go into space
and the moon is in space
a pancake is in space
there are aliens in space
there is a horse in space
there are all sorts of things in space.

Sarah Branton (8)
Burnham Copse Junior School

PANCAKE DAY IN SPACE

Pancake Day, Pancake Day
every year in that space.
Everybody is always happy
'cause it's always pancakes
pancakes, pancakes, pancakes.
Flying saucer in space
I wish I was an astronaut
because I could fly in the sky
and in the space as well and
fly across the planet.

Paul Fell (8)
Burnham Copse Junior School

HOPPING IN SPACE

Hopping in space,
Looking face to face,
With an alien on the Milky Way,
And he just happened to say,
Hello to me,
I said he was jolly kind,
And if you don't mind,
I'll have to say,
Bye bye to the Milky Way.

Guy Grimshawe (9)
Burnham Copse Junior School

IN SPACE

One day I ran into a big meadow,
I was playing in the field.
Then suddenly an alien's ship
Speeded down from the sky and
Through a pie and it landed
In my brother's face.
When the ship landed, my friends ran away.
Then I went 'Hey!' Then an alien grabbed me.
Then the ship took off to space with me inside.
I saw an alien coming.

Thomas Ridley (8)
Burnham Copse Junior School

SPACE ALIENS

I was an alien from earth
but now I'm up in space
but now I'm in Star Wars
fighting enemy
I killed a nasty monster
now I killed another monster
and I killed a teacher from earth
it was in here
and then someone killed me.

Mark Snell (7)
Burnham Copse Junior School

SPACE PANCAKE DAY

On Pancake Day in space
all the space aliens were excited
because they were going to a party
and when they got there they were
stuffing their faces with pancakes
and nobody had any food left.
So the party was called off
and when they got back
they all got told off
and the other aliens fell asleep.

Jonathan Gray (7)
Burnham Copse Junior School

THE MILKY WAY

A plane I say! A Milky Way
Flying through the sky. 'Are you sure?'
'I'm sure OK.'
'I don't believe you.'
'You don't have to.'
'Don't I, that's good.'
'OK I take that as you don't believe me?'
'No I don't.'
'OK bye.'

Chloe Martin (8)
Burnham Copse Junior School

I'M A GRANNY ASTRONAUT

I'm a granny astronaut
And I'm 101.
I have a friend and she is very dumb.
One day it was Pancake Day.
We made a pancake out of clay
And put tomato sauce in it,
And creepy crawlies in it
And it made me very sick,
And it turned me into an
Alien.

Jessica Skinner (7)
Burnham Copse Junior School

LONELINESS

My lips have kissed the horizon,
And my life has fallen into darkness.
I am locked in a cell,
I have fallen into a cave.
When I needed my friends, I found I was all alone.
Even the light coming through my window
Brings sadness and gloom.
There may be a sun in the world,
But if so then I am as good as blind.
From the fun I used to have in the fields,
To my dark cove in the streets,
There isn't a friend to find.
The day getting darker to night.
The light of my life will never rise,
Instead it will die in darkness.

Amy Keighley (10)
Oakley CE Junior School

A Teen Girl!

There she stands cool and relaxed,
With bright make-up jumping out at you,
Her platform shoes 8cm high.

Never ever time for homework,
Always time for shopping,
Blue and purple nails beaming at you,
Ears pierced 3 times on each ear.

Horrible mood swings,
Bad language all the time,
Loud and full of energy,
Plays music disturbingly loud.

Dyed hair in a wacky style,
Chatting up any boy who comes along,
Chewing gum loudly,
Arrives home an hour late.

Lucy Harris (11)
Preston Candover CE Primary School

Snail

A short, stout snail,
Slowly slithered, slimily across the slate.
Suddenly,
Someone squashed the short, stout, slimy
Snail.
Squish!

James Dumelow (10)
Preston Candover CE Primary School

MATHS

Multiply, times, divide, plus,
What on earth do they all mean?
What is the hair root (or is it square root),
Of five thousand and thirteen?

They think we all know the answers,
Of all the sums that they provide,
We say we know the answers,
We lied!

Our teacher's really old,
We call her 'Granny Mable',
She goes out and comes in to find,
We've fainted on the table!

400 sums in twenty minutes,
'Impossible' we say,
We couldn't do 400 sums,
In half a day!

At the end of maths,
We go out to play,
Thank goodness we don't have to do maths,
Until another day.

Christopher Gillman (11)
Preston Candover CE Primary School

THROUGH THE STARS

Flying through the stars,
The Earth, the Moon and Mars.
Whizzing through the Milky Way,
Landing in a spaceship's docking bay.

Inside a spaceship soaring through space,
Looking down on the human race.
In a space suit floating around,
But floating in what? *Nothing!*

Thomas Cole (10)
Preston Candover CE Primary School

SORROW

Close all the curtains,
Lock all the doors,
As we mourn, mourn, mourn,
My life is torn,
I lie in bed awake sometimes,
Thinking about the past,
I find it so, so harsh,
Oh! What will I do without thee,
My heart is broken,
My blood is sour,
I have no power at this hour,
All I hear is a breath of wind,
And a hurried bat,
My life is torn and dead,
Close all the curtains,
Lock all the doors,
As we mourn, mourn, mourn.

Rebecca Bennett (10)
Preston Candover CE Primary School

WHY DID YOU DIE GEORGE?

Black out the sky,
Paint the clouds dark grey,
He left me!
Why?

Why he left me nobody knows,
We were sorry you died,
He left me!
Why?

He left me on the day I hate,
He was a lovely man to know,
He left me!
Why?

James Silvester (10)
Preston Candover CE Primary School

TO FIGS MY CAT

I love you though you ran away.
I love you though you always scratched.
I love you though you went away and I only saw you next day.
I love you though you killed mice and left them on the landing.
I love you though I'll never see you again.
I love you I do.

Gemma Cumberlidge (10)
Preston Candover CE Primary School

MOURNING

He once was a brave character playing his part in life,
But then was struck down by dagger and by knife.
Then came a tragic time at the racecourse that day,
When happy memories stopped their play.
That was when the mourners came,
With their sadness and sorrow to proclaim.
Each with a plentiful bouquet,
Or sad things to say.
Panting mouths and heavy lungs running to see,
A loving body being bundled away in a locked van
                                    no trace of the key.
That night the haynet was empty, the hooves didn't clatter,
Because the loss of a horse is the one thing that would matter.

Daisy Smith (10)
Preston Candover CE Primary School

SADNESS

Sorry Pebbles, you had to die,
Every time I think of you I cry,
I loved to ride you, really I did.

You were such fun,
You used to glisten in the sun,
I love you Pebbles, really I do.

Charlotte Jackson-Stott (10)
Preston Candover CE Primary School

I DREAM OF A PLACE

I dream of a place in a valley, with a
river where swim
the fish
and the kingfishers dive.
Swallows flitting round and round,
the house is built of stone, and heavily thatched,
with ten latticed windows.

The ducks, blue tits and great tits come by
day, with robins and sparrows.

There are fields and fields of
wild flowers droning with the bee.

Peter Wheelwright (10)
Preston Candover CE Primary School

THERE ONCE WAS A SAILOR

Climbing the sails, washing the decks,
Hating every hour, dreading the next.
Frightening waves, threatening his life,
So close to death, missing his wife.
Hungry and sore, needing a drink,
Worrying that the ship is going to sink.
Being bossed about, being kept above,
Always knowing he was a long, long way from *love!*

Tiggy Grafton (9)
Preston Candover CE Primary School

NEW YEAR RESOLUTIONS

I will not feed my dog under the table.
I'll clean my teeth every night.
I'll go to school without hesitation
and get As most times.
I'll do the washing up and scrub
the plates till they nearly crack up.
I'll only use a drop of ketchup
instead of my usual amount.
I'll clean my shoes every night.
I'll let my brother in my bedroom
he can pick up anything he wants!
Yeah right!

Frances Swithinbank (10)
Preston Candover CE Primary School

THE WIND AND THE WOLF

The wind is a wolf,
Howling through the forest,
Speedily whipping across the countryside,
Biting cold.

The wolf is the wind,
Soft and gentle at times,
Fast as a gale,
Wild and ferocious.

Sarah Bowden (10)
Preston Candover CE Primary School

WINDS OF RAGE

An argument with the
winds of rage.

Lashing with every crash of a wave.
The cold weather freezes between
every friendship.

Strong waves -
strong opinions.

Falling out punches large holes in the
rock of friendship.
The violent waves strike hurtful blows.

Mark East (11)
Preston Candover CE Primary School

POEM

'Class, today we're going to write a poem!' the teacher says,
I'm trying to think,
And she says 'Stop messing around,
And get on with your work.'

'This poem is hard' I said to my mate,
'And they've done 50 lines already!'

Then you have to do it at play time,
I'm sure you know what I mean!

Ian Simpson (11)
Preston Candover CE Primary School

ANGER

It started to bubble inside me.
My head was hot and sticky.
I had to get my hands on him,
But how?
He'd better keep out of my way because
Any minute now my bubbles are going to burst.
I should rip him into tiny shreds.
I could give him worse that that!
I know, I will trick him,
No, that wouldn't work.
Will I ever get my hands on him before my bubbles burst!

Polly Barker (9)
Preston Candover CE Primary School

NEW YEAR RESOLUTIONS

Wash every day,
Clean my teeth,
Comb my hair,
Get up early,
Feed my pet,
And go to bed early.
It's a long, long, list but
Is it worth it?

Of course not!

Carl Lintott (11)
Preston Candover CE Primary School

CITY LIFE

Lorries running by,
Smoke puffing in the grey sky.
Skyscrapers stand high.

People in the shops,
Dressed in blue are all the cops,
Traffic jams, cars stop.

Old ladies' dogs bark,
Children running in the park,
Lights on in the dark.

Joanna Travis (9)
Preston Candover CE Primary School

THE MILKY WAY

We are in the Milky Way,
A tiny part,
But
Our sun is still a giant,
A big ball of flaming gas.
Hotter than a nuclear explosion,
White,
Blinding light,
Without it blackness,
Pitch-black,
Cold,
Quiet.

Stephan Randall (8)
St Neot's School, Hook

NOVEMBER NIGHT

The snap of twigs,
The crunch of the frost,
The darkness of night,
The light has been lost.

Whoosh goes the rocket,
Flying in the air,
Boom goes the gunpowder,
Exploding in the air.

All bright colours,
Red, green, blue flares,
Fill the land in light,
In the deep, deep blue air.

The heat of the bonfire,
Crackling and fizzing,
Burning the air,
A source of lighting.

November night,
Is prickly and cold,
November night,
Is dark and old.

Andrew MacDonald (11)
St Neot's School, Hook

SPRING IN THE MORNING

Bright sun streams through the window,
Everyone taking life slow,
Birds all sing,
As they flap their wings,
Birds fly,
In bright turquoise sky,
Water trickles over pebbles in the stream,
Sun shines down in golden beams,
Frost gleams in the sun,
Horses canter in the field having great fun,
Riding ponies over log jumps,
Near the bushes that grow in clumps,
Tiny fawns trying to stand,
While their brothers and sisters leap across the land,
That's my idea of a spring morning.

Katie Reeves (10)
St Neot's School, Hook

SPRING

The countryside is awakening,
Spring is on its way.
Leaves bursting on trees again,
Yellow and green flowers pushing
Through the cold ground.
Baby animals,
Baby birds,
New life,
Lighter mornings, lighter evenings,
Summer to look forward to.

Rebecca Harman (7)
St Neot's School, Hook

MISSION IS POSSIBLE

The ant colony, Ayers Rock.
An army jittering along,
Creeping over and under logs.
Courageously,
Venturing through the terrain.
Marching with pride,
Slaughtering anything in their path,
Fearlessly,
Mercilessly,
Single file.
Mission is possible,
Crossing horizons, angry waters,
Object,
Food!

Lawrence Richards (8)
St Neot's School, Hook

THE BLACK NIGHT

The blackest night,
The brightest sun,
Huge,
A glowing ball of gas:
Twinkling stars,
A Milky Way,
A comet whizzes, lightning quick,
Through the dark.
Saturn with her beautiful rings,
A giant moving slowly,
Gold and red.

Oliver Hill (8)
St Neot's School, Hook

MY BEST FRIEND

My best friend is quite like me,
With bright blue eyes, as blue as the sea,
She has lovely blonde hair,
And lovely long nails.
She adores hamsters and gerbils,
But she doesn't like snails.

You see
We are best friends,
'Cos we just seem to be
The same sort of people,
From her to me.

Giverny Gallagher (9)
St Neot's School, Hook

THE RED PLANET

Our solar system begins with -
Our sun,
Burning, gigantic,
Floating in the blackness of space.

The planets smoothly orbiting,
Reflecting light,
A beautiful sight,
Saturn's gold and silver rings,
Our own blue and green Earth
And
The red planet.

Steven Dombkouski (8)
St Neot's School, Hook

THE MIDNIGHT HOUR

I glared around my gran's spare room,
The wind spun through the open windows
and hit me hard on the face,
My heart slowed with fear and my hands began
to shake like branches on a tree,
The door slammed shut and made the old wooden
walls shake and chatter like teeth,
I heard a piercing scream puncture my ear,
I spotted a ghostly shadow creep along the wall,
A big howl ceased the silence,
The stairs creaked grabbing my relaxation
and chucking a bag of fear over me instead,
The moon disappeared under a great black cloud
and the darkness crept over me,
I smelt the dark danger,
I dived for the covers now even more scared than before,
The warmth jumped on me and the sun danced up to
cover me with relaxation,
I smelt the pretty fresh air and heard children playing
games.

Nicole Bunn (9)
Tadley Primary School

ENJOYMENT

Enjoyment has a sweetening taste,
Sounding like a tweetie bird singing down your ears,
Purple is the colour of yellow sparks twinkling out,
Looking like a shooting star bolting past and waving bye bye,
Feeling like a wet sponge dribbling down your face.

Sophie Bevan (8)
Tadley Primary School

SUNDAY

The sun shines on the newly washed car,
People in their gardens digging weeds,
The car slows down as the unknowing child gallops across the road,
An old man sits with wine on the table and book in hand,
A leafless tree stands still,
Spring is on its way.

A sprout of a plant,
The still wind,
The smell of the air,
The singing of the birds,
These are all signs of the same thing,
A sign that says,
Spring is on its way.

A crowd of people ready for a walk,
A dog lays on the growing grass,
All is dead apart from a prowling cat,
As the wind rises the car begins to dry,
The old man is beaten by the chill of the wind,
The birds stop singing,
This is a reminder that it is still winter,
But they all know,
Spring is on the way.

Luke Towey (11)
Tadley Primary School

LOVE

Love is as red as roses
and as pink as pink can be.
It tastes like sweet strawberries
and a pinch of sugar.
Love smells like Cadbury's chocolate.

It looks like heaven
where clouds are what you walk on.
Love sounds like birds singing and swirling
about in the sky.
It feels like velvet and is very nice.

Gemma Louise Matthews (9)
Tadley Primary School

THE SHOUT

The night was dark, the night was still,
nothing moved and nothing will.
Then there was a clunk and the
teleprinter flicked into action.
The lights came on and the bell
started to ring.
The fireman upstairs started to stir
then all of a sudden one jumped up.
Then three and four, there were ten in all.
They slipped on their shoes and
ran to the pole.
They slipped down in order of rank
and were met at the bottom by the
Station Master.
As they came down he gave them
an order and then ran to an engine.
The siren started, the lights gave
a flash and then the bright red engine
disappeared into the dark.
The five that were left went back to bed.
The night was dark, the night was still,
nothing moved and nothing will,
or will it?

James Nicholson (11)
Tadley Primary School

MIDNIGHT

As the sun set,
The sky slowly grew darker
I could hear the rain
Tapping onto the windowpane

As cars pull to a stop
Outside the house
A creak came from the stairs
The wind swirling outside
Made leaves rustle
Cats fighting outside
Made a low hissing
Dogs woofing echoed like
a dolphin swimming in the sea
Two glittering stars
Looked like shining eyes
There was a loud bang
The curtains pulled themselves
open with a creak
The sun shot in
I dived under my covers
But the room was light again.

Micah Bremner (9)
Tadley Primary School

KETCHUP DRACULA

Big, pointy teeth,
Ketchup dropping,
Mum walks in,
I hide behind a bin,
She roars,
'Have you been playing with ketchup Jim?'
I tell the truth to my mum Kim.

I like being a vampire,
I scare all my friends,
They're all wimps,
One of them limps,
I bit his leg that's why.
When I get home,
I have blood pie.

Mark Houchin (10)
Tadley Primary School

THE HAUNTED ROOM

I felt my duvet roll over off my bed
The coldness cut my pale skin
A shiver ran down my spine as the breeze
crept past
Cars tooted as they got nearer
Wails and screams filled my head with terror,
Shadows I could see were dancing to the
wolves howling outside
Tapping on my window made me feel more
nervous than ever,
My clothes looked as though they were
dancing to the midnight moon
The stars looked pale as if they were ill
The door creaked open
I opened my mouth to scream but
nothing came out
My curtains started flapping as I heard
creaking on the stairs,
As dawn came the sounds stopped
I still had the night in the
haunted room in my mind.

Michelle Tomlinson (9)
Tadley Primary School

IN THE MIDDLE OF THE NIGHT

I saw the moon light up the sky,
I saw some glittering stars,
I could see everything you can see in the middle of the night.
I heard the wolves,
I heard the owls,
I heard everything you can hear in the middle of the night.
I saw a shadow dance like a ballerina on my bedroom wall,
I heard the cars go rushing by and hooting as they went.
I saw a black figure rush past my bedroom,
I got out of bed,
I rushed to my door,
Suddenly I heard a shriek.
I fell back,
I felt something that I'd never felt before,
A strong piece of clothing,
A mask, a mask that I couldn't see,
I went back into my bed.
Suddenly I heard some birds that whistled,
I heard the hen that meant night was *over.*

Katie Mackinnon (9)
Tadley Primary School

JOY

Joy is pink,
It is sugar,
It smells like lovely clean socks,
It looks like a lovely bowl of jelly,
It sounds like the leaves blowing in the wind,
It feels like an ice-cream running down my back.

Richard Nash (8)
Tadley Primary School

WHAT IS IT LIKE ON THE MOON?

What is it like on the moon?
The moon is a football
that has been kicked into space.
The moon has a face as big as a comet.
The moon is a pebble in front of my eyes.
I see the shadow of a werewolf in front of my eyes
howling like the wind.
From where it sits in the night sky
the moon looks down upon me.
I close my eyes and try to forget
but the thought echoes through my head.
I try to think it's just a dream,
another echo, oh no it cries *Joshua, Joshua, Joshua.*
It all clears out and I think myself awake.
Phew, I think I closed my eyes and fell asleep.
There sat the moon with a convoy of stars.
It opened its mouth to talk.
Is it a dream, is it worth a scream?
What is it like on the moon?

Joshua Delaney (9)
Tadley Primary School

HAPPINESS

Happiness is yellow,
happiness tastes like pork,
happiness smells like bread,
happiness looks like animals,
happiness sounds like laughter,
happiness feels like joy.

Nick Fletcher (8)
Tadley Primary School

SUMMER

Flowers are blooming about our feet
Daisies are swaying in time to the breeze
The fresh cut grass shining in the sun
The children playing, summer's just begun.

Children screaming, playing catch, limbo, skipping,
What about that?
Brothers crying, playing football just lost
the game, oh so, so bad.

Birds chirping in the sky
Rabbits jumping oh so high
The time of the ice-cream van comes round,
Money jingling in our hands
The ice-cream man so grand and jolly
smiles at us and asks for money.

The splashing of water in the pool causes
a stir and rain starts to fall ranting,
raving everyone runs quick to the shelter, *phew!*

Kayleigh Keen (11)
Tadley Primary School

SADNESS

Sadness tastes like cold rice pudding.
It feels wet.
Sadness sounds like a cold whispering voice.
Its colour is grey.
Sadness smells rotten and old.
Sadness looks rusty.

Jack Lewis (9)
Tadley Primary School

IT WASN'T ME

What broken vase?
What shattered window?
It wasn't me,
I didn't do it.

Who pushed Jenny in the lake?
It wasn't me,
I didn't do it.

Who ate the bread all fresh and new?
It wasn't me, I didn't do it.

Who scared the cat
And kicked the dog?
It wasn't me,
I didn't do it.

I know you did those awful things.
It wasn't me,
I did do it! (Oops!)

Rebecca Simpson (11)
Tadley Primary School

LOVE

Pink is the colour of love.
Love tastes like strawberries.
It smells of sugar and spice.
Love looks like a beautiful heart.
Kissing sound is of beautiful love.
Smooth is the power of love.

Abby Vincent (9)
Tadley Primary School

SHIVERING

Shivering like an engine rotating
with the covers right over my head.
Cats outside were hissing
and fighting and screeching.
Suddenly the silence fell on the street again.
Shadows rose from under my bed
and started creeping around.
My window flew open
and slammed shut
like a bottle smashing
on the ground.
Then out of the corner of my eye
a bony finger slipped round my door.
I dared think about what it might be.
I dived back under my covers
now even more scared and now
the shivering was like an earthquake
waiting to erupt.

Abigail King (8)
Tadley Primary School

LOVE

Love is red covered with roses.
Love is the taste of strawberries.
Love smells of a really sweet flower.
Love is the shape of a heart.
Love sounds like birds singing.
Love is so soft.

Mereasa Boyes (8)
Tadley Primary School

EXCITEMENT

Excitement is a bright yellow.
Its taste is fruit salad,
smelling of bananas,
and looking like a flower.
Its sound is like a fairy bell,
it's a lovely feeling for me.

Charlotte Green (9)
Tadley Primary School

SADNESS

The colour is dark blue,
Sadness is plain and watery,
The smell of sadness is plain,
Dullness is the look,
The sound of sadness is crying,
The feel is one all on his own.

Bradley Hill (9)
Tadley Primary School

EXCITEMENT

Excited is the colour of a rainbow,
It tastes of sweet fresh strawberries,
It smells of a sweet smelling incense,
Excited looks like a pony trotting around a field,
It sounds like a bird singing away,
It feels like a puppy sleeping on a rug.

Victoria Kyle (8)
Tadley Primary School

MIDNIGHT MOON

My door slammed shut
I could see the moon out of my bedroom window
The patterns on my ceiling were gleaming in the moonlight
There were shadows jumping all over the walls
I could hear the tap dripping in the bathroom
The neighbours' cats were hissing and fighting
A police car drove by, its sirens hit my ears
I could feel myself shaking, terribly
But I felt safe feeling the warm comfort of my bed
My pillow was soft and very inviting
But then came a bang
A scent of fuel flew up my nose as a motorbike shot past
The smell of burning came from the allotment
It was as if people were dancing round me
This night was turning into a nightmare
Suddenly I knew I was alone
My hot water bottle went cold
And I hid my head under the cover.

Kate Turner (9)
Tadley Primary School

THE SURPRISE

Red is the colour for surprise,
It tastes of sugar and spice and
it's quite nice,
It smells like strawberries in a dish,
It looks like a cute guinea pig,
Surprise sounds like a cooking pot,
Surprise feels very jolly inside me.

Chloë Meakes (9)
Tadley Primary School

THE NIGHT

The stars are bright in the moonlit sky
As I look out of my window,
There is a moving object on the floor,
I hear a car rumbling to a stop,
I can smell the oil from the back of the car,
The television's blaring downstairs,
I smell a smell of dirty mud,
I'm very tired and sleepy as I lie in
my bed,
I hear people chatting,
I smell some food from downstairs,
The wind is howling outside,
I feel scared and very worried,
The rain is rapping on the window,
I hear some cats screaming outside,
A big bright light is shining in the sky,
I hear car radios going on,
It all goes quiet and I fall asleep.

Charlotte Townsend (8)
Tadley Primary School

MAD AS A HATTER

It tastes of rotten cheese.
It also sounds like your voice
when you fall down a pit.
It looks like people mad as a hatter.
It also feels like sandpaper.
The colour is black.
It smells of steam.

Mark Osborne (9)
Tadley Primary School

OUTSIDE

The tapping on the window grew louder
Wolves were howling outside
Creaking on the stairs grew nearer
Someone was on the landing
Its eyes were shining like headlights
Shouting and screaming could be
heard under my window
Someone or something was creeping
across my landing
I was imagining that all the shadows
were creeping in closer
I could feel something slimy
at the end of my bed
I was also imagining that a witch
was outside my window
I never knew what was on my landing
Or was it my imagination?

James Miller (8)
Tadley Primary School

LOVE

Red is the colour of love.
Strawberries are the best for
the wonderful love.
The smell of love is really sweet.
The shape is heart.
The sound is sort of wavy.
The feel of love is soft.

Rebecca Hamer (9)
Tadley Primary School

DARKNESS

The moon is round and yellow like the sun
Shadows creeping across the room
Stars like fireflies
Sound of footsteps running away
Leaves rustling in the wind
Dogs barking at strangers
I imagine a goblin under my bed
A ghost eating my socks
A ghost was scratching on the door
A scorpion's on my bed
Hot and sweaty in the bed
Smell the cold air of night
The rubbish dump smells
And the bin from downstairs
Smell the food downstairs
The clock strikes twelve as
Midnight comes.

Rachael Dolan (9)
Tadley Primary School

ANGER

Anger is as black as the night.
Anger tastes of blood.
Anger smells of gas.
It looks like a tear in a shirt.
Anger sounds like shouts and cries.
It feels as painful as someone stabbing
you in the back.

Ben Bennett (9)
Tadley Primary School

THE NIGHT THAT I WAS SCARED

I was sitting there shivering until my heart stopped
I saw this shadow
It was creeping around my room
I was seeing rats
I could see shooting stars running across the sky
I could hear snoring
I could hear mice squeaking
I could smell the air coming through my window
A gust of wind went in
Whoosh
Now I was breathtaken
Then I felt a tickle on my leg
The downstairs door opened and shut
It was my dad from work
Bang
The window opened and shut
The sun rose up it was morning.

Abby-Jade Nicholas (9)
Tadley Primary School

A BIG SURPRISE

Surprised is the colour of a daffodil
drifting in the breeze.
It tastes like a birthday cake with people singing
happy birthday to you.
It smells like sweet perfume drifting up your nose.
It looks like a big present wrapped in pretty paper
and surprised feels like a Christmas tree.

Lauren Thompson (9)
Tadley Primary School

WILDLIFE

Consider the wildlife,
The birds and bees,
Yes look after it,
Both you and me.

The animals that get killed,
Just for man's greed,
Please listen,
Consider its need.

With all the pollution,
We need a solution,
To keep the animals alive.

So don't dump the rubbish,
Catch the bus,
Think of them
And not just us.

Iain Lock (11)
Tadley Primary School

THE HORRIBLE NIGHT

When I go to bed at night,
My room fills up with light,
Monsters creeping and leaping up to my height.
I keep my eyes shut and squeeze them tight
So nothing can frighten me at all.
I try and tighten my eyes,
Up to the end of the night.
That's all.

Katie Lockyer (11)
Tadley Primary School

LOVE

Love is the colour of
kiss red.
Love tastes sweet and it
bubbles in your mouth.

Love smells of strawberries
sweet and cool.

Love looks like a bright
red rose.

Love sounds bright
and clear.

Love feels soft and
silky, rubbing on you.

Love is life.

April Bogue (9)
Tadley Primary School

A BLACK CAT WITH A HAT

There once was a black cat with a very fishy hat.
The black cat always wears the very old fishy hat,
even when someone strokes him they think he looks
quite cute,
but when he scratches he is not very cute anymore.

He always waits for food on the doorstep and even at
home.
But he never gets food but sometimes he does.
He's the cat with the fishy old hat.

Michael Flitter (10)
Tadley Primary School

WINDY NIGHTS

I was stone-cold in my bed
I could hear mice squeaking downstairs
A big shadow crept across my wall
It was very quiet until *bang!*
Plates crashed off the shelf
I imagined a nightmare coming on
I imagined a robber coming in,
I was feeling ill
My door slammed shut
The moon shone through
Bats squawking
The night went on with the same sounds
Then I had enough and screamed
My mummy and daddy came in
And I felt safe and secure.

Matthew Jones (8)
Tadley Primary School

MY MOTHER

My mother says
'Eat that now before it gets cold.'
She gives me peas
that taste like fleas
and mushy steak
like chocolate cake.
She gives me carrots
that taste like parrots
and she gives me a pear
just like a hare.

Danny Nicholas (10)
Tadley Primary School

THAT NIGHT

As the moon lit up the lofty sky,
I saw a twinkle of the yellow star.
Someone ran through the darkness of the forest,
I had a shiver down my spine,
I heard the cars rushing on the track.
Me shivering in my cosy bed,
The swooshing trees at the window,
The owl hooting, *hoot, hoot,*
Cats fighting, *kee, kee,*
The wind whistling in my ear,
Shadows creeping up my wall,
Lights zooming past my wall,
The smell of cooking in the air,
My teddy falling flat, *boink,*
So that night I got scared.

Victoria Wagstaff (8)
Tadley Primary School

SHADOWS

My shadow copies me,
It runs when I run,
It walks when I walk,
When I move it moves too.
It's like people at school,
They copy their friends,
And off the blackboard too.

I just think it's a copycat.
Maybe if there was no sun,
There'd be no shadow to copy me.

Kay Goff (11)
Tadley Primary School

NIGHT-TIME

As the moon shimmered brightly
The stars twinkled like cats' eyes
Every tree looked like a monster
against the night
The floorboards creaked and groaned
I could hear doors creaking and groaning
inside the house
Owls hooted, cats screeched
The wind was howling around me
I felt the branches scratching me
I could smell the leftover bonfire smoke
from next door
I could imagine what was happening
in the rest of the world
I was very happy.

Mark Fussey (9)
Tadley Primary School

THE SCARY NIGHT

The moon glittered in the ebony sky,
Howls fly through your head.
Yellow circles zoom past your window.
You see spooky outlines.
Nasty red eyes glare into yours.
Shadows on the wall make your eyes open wide.
You imagine monsters under your bed.
Musty smells fill your nose.
You hear creaks as the door moves open and shut.
You imagine vampires,
You dare not move.

Rowan Duncan Arthur (9)
Tadley Primary School

SCHOOL HOMEWORK

When you feel free,
you get even more.
Homework, homework,
the worst thing in the world.
Homework, the dreaded word.
English, maths, geography, history,
the list never ends.

If you don't do it,
goodness knows what happens to you.
You plan things
and then you've got more.
So do your homework
and then you can
have some fun!

Sarah Eaves (11)
Tadley Primary School

A SCARY POEM

The house was silent.
Shadows of the moon,
Shadows were dancing,
Tapping on the windows.
The wind was howling,
Wolves were howling.
People running away from the graveyard.
Something was scratching in my bed.
Mice were running across my bedroom.
People crying out said,
'I can smell fish and chips.'

Calum Douglas (8)
Tadley Primary School

THE HAUNTED NIGHT

I saw the trees moving
I heard the trees whistling
The birds flew past my window
The cars rushed past my window
Tooting as they went
I heard my sister screaming
I began to shout
The curtains puffed out
My bedroom light went off
I saw a spider climbing up me
My sister shut up
I got to sleep at last
I woke up again
The sun was shining.

Kylie Boyce (8)
Tadley Primary School

JANICE THE PIG

Janice the pig came out to play,
said hello and ran away.
We never knew where she went
perhaps it was down south to Kent.
We chased her for a mile
but lost her at the River Nile.
We wandered back home that day
feeling far from gay.
We bought a new pig,
in bed I thought *he's as green as a fig.*
Then he ran away and
the whole procedure was on the following day.

Chris Boardman (10)
Tadley Primary School

GALLOPING HORSE

The chestnut gallops across the field,
His coat glistening in the sun,
Sweat pouring down his head,
But still he gallops on.

He glides across the luscious grass,
Jumps the wooden fence,
His muscular legs getting weary
But still he gallops on.

He quickly comes to a standstill,
For in front of him,
Some noisy monsters rushing past,
The road has halted him.

Matthew Bunn (11)
Tadley Primary School

IN THE DARKNESS

The house stood silently when the clock loudly struck twelve.
I heard something tap softly on the window sill.
And I heard the wind howl painfully.
I pulled back the curtains and looked.
I could see the rain falling as fast as a train when it's in a hurry.
I could see the trees being blown in the howling wind.
I could see cars with shining lights like cats' eyes
                    speeding through the darkness.
I heard the owls twitting from a long distance away.
Something black flew across the sky, it looked like a bat.
Suddenly I heard the screech of a cry, it sounded like cats fighting.
Then the curtain fell back and I fell into a deep, deep sleep.

Katherine Birkinshaw (9)
Tadley Primary School

SECRETS

I've got a secret,
As secret as can be,
The secret belongs to one person,
That secret person is me.

At night I think of my secret,
In day I think some more,
My friends want to know my secret,
It makes me rather sore.

I've got a secret,
As secret as can be,
The secret belongs to one person,
That secret person is me.

Lucy Boxall (11)
Tadley Primary School

ON THE MOON

On the moon in dark, dark space
On a planet big and round
Shining bright and colour white
Like a globe glowing bright
Rocket sounds going there
A creature making a noise
The moon hovering up in space
In that pitch-black sky
In the holes deep, deep down
Brown and stiff
On my way back home
Sleeping tight
Snoring hard into bed.

Ashley Deller-Merricks (8)
Tadley Primary School

THE GRAVEYARD

It was midnight
Wolves were howling
I was shivering and it smelt disgusting
With all the dead people
I wished I was in bed
Then the wind skidded across the ground
I jumped up because it was going to
knock me over
Then the leaves flew back up
and they hooked onto the sharp branches
Then the church bells rang
Then everything went quiet
Then I saw a bird hanging from a branch.

Alex Menicou (8)
Tadley Primary School

THE MOON

The moon is a white clock
that comes out at night.
It is like a snowflake,
that floats lightly in space.
It is like a smooth plate,
waiting to have food on.
It makes a crumbling noise,
like a cliff breaking up.
It moves slowly and steadily
like an aeroplane in the sky.
At night it glistens brightly,
like a sparkly ball.

Joanna Pearce (11)
Winklebury Junior School

THE MOON

The moon is white chalk
Writing across the blackboard.
It is bleak and cold,
Like ice cubes, cold and white.

The moon sounds like the ocean, swaying lightly,
Or a beating drum
Lightly tapping,
Tapping against the wood.

The moon, slowly turning,
Like car wheels on a bumpy beach.
It's like a seal,
Swimming in the dark,
Or like an elephant
Stomping around and around.

Zakeera Suffee (11)
Winklebury Junior School

METEORITE

Rocky and circular,
Like a clock face
Until they explode.

Like a big, juicy plum,
Just about to be crunched,
Zooming until it gets crushed
And all worn out.

A meteorite is a heart,
Beating faster and faster
Until it suddenly stops.

Vincent Bugg (10)
Winklebury Junior School

THE SUN

The sun is like a fireball,
Standing in the deep, dark woods.
A football kicked high
In the black night sky.
A golden plate
Floating up into space.
An explosion of colourful gases,
Trapped in a see-through ball.
Sounds like cooking pancakes,
When you get up close.

The sun,
  A fireball,
    A flying football,
      A golden plate,
        And an explosion of gases.

Oliver Pullein (9)
Winklebury Junior School

THE SUN

The sun is like a lion,
Roaring with flames.
It's like a tennis ball,
Gliding through the air.
It sounds like a bonfire,
Spitting out flames.
It moves like a snail,
Twirling around the galaxy.
The sun is golden,
Like a ring that spins.
It's like a massive, humungous orange.

Sheryl Wild (11)
Winklebury Junior School

COSMIC POEM

That night sitting on my bed
Staring at the black night sky
Thinking to myself sitting on my bed
I thought I was floating then *suddenly!*
There I was flying in space.

I decided to have a ride on the Milky Way.
I went through Mars.
I went all the way through, suddenly
I started to get cold,
Realised I had gone out of the universe.

When I woke up
I was relieved.
I never had sat on my bed
At night and stared
Through my window because I was so scared.

Stephanie Bowles (9)
Winklebury Junior School

THE MOON

Look up there,
There's a pie in the sky.
No, it's a ball,
And it's going to fall.

It's silent, so silent.
It's like a seal, so high, so still.
It looks like a white crystal,
Glistening in the sky,
Up so high.

Louise Burt (10)
Winklebury Junior School

COSMIC POEM

I'm here at last,
I'm floating, drifting in the air.
Planets, oxygen, suddenly *bang*
What was *th-a-a-a-t*?

Oh no I'm in the black hole,
I'm on a space rope at least,
To be pulled back in ten minutes,
I might as well explore.

It's a whole new galaxy I've found,
When we get back to Earth
I will be famous.

There's a blue sun, a yellow sky,
Purple grass, green sea and red fish.
I'm back in the galaxy again now.

Cool, there's Pluto and Mars, Venus,
Mercury and Uranus, Jupiter and Saturn.
See you, bye!

Lauren Austin (9)
Winklebury Junior School

THE MOON

The moon is a silver milk bottle top.
It is cold on one side
and warm on the other.
You can hear the tinkle of moon rocks
hitting the stars.
The moon moves like a tennis ball
that has just been hit.

Jonathan Crook (10)
Winklebury Junior School

THE BLACK HOLE

5, 4, 3, 2, 1, *lift off.*
Hey look at this, we're up in space.
Look at this, we've landed in a crater.
Look up there, there's the black hole.
Now guess what, we've just broken down.

Look there's a comet, it's landed on Mars,
Bang!
Oh no there's an alien,
It's come over here.

Look at all those spaceships
And the moon buggies.
Oh no I've lost my gravity,
What shall I do now?

We'd better fix the engine
Or we'll never get back home.
Mum will be worried
And then she might *faint!*

Rachel Harris (9)
Winklebury Junior School

THE GLITTERING MOON

The glittering moon
in the dark blue sky.
Crackling, sizzling, *boom.*
Yellow, creamy white,
the colour of the moon.
The moon is like a silver ball
turning in the sky.

Vicky Lemm (11)
Winklebury Junior School

THROUGH THE BLACK HOLE

5, 4, 3, 2, 1, lift off
Planets zooming by
The Milky Way is very high,
Moon buggy, bumpy, bumpy.

Oh no, an asteroid field
Better get out of it quick
Why I am in all of a mix
I need to fix all of my problems quick.

Watch all the stars tonight
What a very pretty sight
We are light years away
When we went through that black hole today.

Emma Johnson (8)
Winklebury Junior School

ASTEROID BELT

Bang, my spaceship goes *swoosh*
through the galaxy past the Milky Way.
Here we go past the planets.
We have been going for a million light years.
Aliens floating past I hear them saying
what a strange sight they were.
One was bold, one was strangely ugly.
What a strange sight they were.
Asteroids floating past at speeds you
couldn't dream of.
Here we go in our small ship.
We're floating round getting dizzy.
That's the end of this wacky poem.

Mark Frost (8)
Winklebury Junior School

MY TRIP TO SPACE

5, 4, 3, 2, 1, *blast-off*!
Oh no it's broken down.
Get in that one,
Off we *gooo*.

We're heading into space
Hooray, hooray
We're heading into space
Horray, hooray, hooray.

Arrr it's an alien
It's come to eat me up
Heeelp!
The aliens seemed to be our friends.

They helped us out of our spaceship,
And called us *boring*.
I felt a little bit silly.
Then aliens took us to Pluto,
And there was a dog.
He was freezing cold,
His head was old
And he smelt like a rotten banana.

I could smell it through the door.
Phew it stinks
I'm staying in here thanks.
Why? Because it *stinks!*
That's why.

I didn't want to go home,
But I tell you
That dog *did* stink,
So I suppose that will be
A very good weekend diary!

Michelle Selina Long (9)
Winklebury Junior School

THE PLANET MARS

I landed on Mars,
Next to some bars.
Aliens came from all directions, looking puzzled.
No explanation to give for a spaceship landing
without permission from Martian HQ.
Suddenly all the aliens ran away
It was my turn to be puzzled.
Bang!
A flying saucer had crashed.
Then I saw a spaceship in orbit.
It pulled the wreck up.
Time to leave Mars with the bars.
10, 9, 8, 7, 6, 5, 4, 3, 2, 1,
Blast-off!

Tim Pearce (9)
Winklebury Junior School

SPACE IS SCARY

Bang!
   Bang! We landed.
I didn't want to get out.
I looked out of the window,
All I could see was little aliens
jumping up and down.
They were making me dizzy.
I went to get a drink of water,
my mouth was as dry as a bone.
I could see the solar system
from where I was standing.
In the end it was time to go home.

Daniel Dorling (8)
Winklebury Junior School

ALIENS ON MARS

5, 4, 3, 2, 1, we have *blast-off!*
We're in space *whooshing* past the stars,
Floating in our spaceship,
We are heading for Mars.

We have landed on Mars and
There are aliens, yes aliens and
They're all looking at the beautiful stars.

We are leaping, leaping very high,
It's good to be able to see the black sky,
There are craters, big craters,
Aaghh! Phew, I nearly fell down one.

There are things that look like train tracks,
They're not their alien footprints,
Do aliens have feet?
Oh yes, I just saw one.

Let's get back now,
We have the evidence,
We have lots of photographs,
They look excellent.

We're back on Earth,
I'll see you next time
We're visiting Pluto!

Terri Leanne Russell (9)
Winklebury Junior School

MOTHER SPACESHIP

I was *whooshing* in space,
Along came an alien
Who said 'Hello, Earthling!'
'Arrrr, monster!' I said.
I was drifting
To a black hole
A different dimension awaits me.

I landed on a planet,
A big one in fact.
I think it was Saturn,
I didn't know for a fact!
There were craters and holes.
The alien was beside me,
I didn't know,
I didn't see the spacecraft.

He zapped me,
I laughed and laughed, it tickled.
I zoomed back to Earth!

Paul Budge (9)
Winklebury Junior School

A STAR

A silver star
is a piece of silver paper,
a small silver snowflake in the sky.
A star is like a silver spaceship,
going slow in the sky,
high above the rainbow,
gliding.

Laura Spiers (10)
Winklebury Junior School

THE STRANGEST PLANET I'VE SEEN

We're taking off,
I hope I've not forgotten
that in book five,
aliens are alive!
It is really weird, I don't know why
but shooting stars are flying by.
There were five of us,
but one got run over by a bus.
Look, a green thing in the distance,
the planet might be called resistance.
Oh help! We're shocked.
Make sure all the doors are locked.
We're going to land
so please hold my hand.
We've landed at last,
I take a big gasp
at all the aliens there are.
Oh help I'm in trouble,
will they eat me?
Just let me be!
This really is a strange planet,
but I think it is the strangest planet I've seen!

Katie Clewley (10)
Winklebury Junior School

MY ALIEN

My alien has
two bright eyes
and two small eyes.
Two long arms
and two small arms.

Natalie Spiers (8)
Winklebury Junior School

STAR TREK VOYAGE AND A HALF

5-4-3-2-1 - blast-off! Shouts Star Machine,
Take that pilot away, he's mean.
Ay ay Scotty, some people say,
Blasting through the Milky Way.
Uh-oh there's a UFO,
Uh-oh it's blasting silky snow.
Snow in space it doesn't make sense,
Snow in space 'Up-Defence'
Let's make a world up there in space,
We'll have plenty to do and lots of aliens to face.
Heavy cargo that there's no need for,
Don't even have to bring that door.
We've landed, yes, it is so great,
Or maybe we've landed in a crate.
There are aliens out in space,
I don't want to see their ugly face.
Meteors are crashing against our sides,
Planets are bashing against our thighs.
That was in my dreams, it was great fun,
Maybe there's something in my bun.
Uh-oh there's a funny look on my face,
Do you know where I'm going tomorrow,
        Out in space!

Richard Reece (9)
Winklebury Junior School

GREEN MEAN ALIENS

Green mean *aliens*, yellow mean *aliens*,
Blue mean *aliens*, red mean *aliens*,
They come from everywhere,
Small *aliens*, big *aliens*,
Fat *aliens*, thin *aliens*,
But all are mean!

Green mean *aliens,* yellow mean *aliens,*
Blue mean *aliens,* red mean *aliens,*
They smell horrid,
They sound like dolphins
They feel rough,
Green mean *aliens*

Lloyd Blackman (11)
Winklebury Junior School

BREAKDOWN

10 . . . 9 . . . 8 . . . 7 . . . 6 . . . 5 . . . 4 . . . 3 . . . 2 . . . 1 . . . Blast-off,
I'm leaving the planet,
I can't see my house,
Only the tall skyscrapers,
I am heading for a planet,
What's the matter with these controls? I scream.
I'm going round and round,
   . . . Crash . . . Bang . . . Boom . . .
My spacecraft is out of control
and there is nothing I can do.
I'm waiting, I'm waiting.
Why am I waiting?
There's no one here of course,
Suddenly I hear a noise going *gwrly, gwrly, gooy goo,*
An alien . . . what am I to do?
I can't call for help,
I'm dead, I'm dead,
I close my eyes . . . but nothing happens,
   . . . I open my eyes . . .
What are you doing?
Suddenly I realised they had fixed my ship,
When I got back I was ready to tell the story,
But unfortunately I woke up.

Kirstie Prior (9)
Winklebury Junior School

UFO Is Here To Grow

UFO is here to grow.
Flying through the air,
the aliens say, it's not fair
with them in there.
We own space,
they should not put in their ugly face.
In space we should be there
controlling the air.
Why! we should do something about this.
Like what?
Give them a shot
and blow up their spaceship.
The spacemen say let's go that way.
No! that way!
OK that way.
I will lay for a day.
Tell me when it's over.
I will turn over and get up.
Let's go to Earth when it's my birthday.
No, we are staying and playing.
Look at those aliens
trying to blow up our spaceship
with lollipops.
What, no way I want to play
that's the way.

Sam Ayres (10)
Winklebury Junior School

UP IN SPACE

I went up to space,
It was a horrible place,
I did not like it at all,
I thought I would fall,
Suddenly we landed,
Of course, I do not know where,
Maybe it was Pluto, maybe it was Mars?
Maybe we just hit one of the stars!
Yes, we have landed,
We landed on the moon,
I hope we do not stay long,
I want to be back by noon.
I have got on my spacesuit,
'Cos I want to go outside,
Do I look like a flyer?
Help, I do not want to go any higher!
We are going down,
Down, back to Earth,
I want to go again some day,
Some day, I hope it is soon,
Next time, can we go to Mars?
Or can we go to a planet,
Way beyond those stars?
I hope you come again sometime,
Just to pick me up,
Googly, googly, giggly, gogly, gluck!

Victoria Englefield (9)
Winklebury Junior School

BLAST-OFF TO MARS

10, 9, 8, 7, 6, 5, 4, 3, 2, 1, blast-off!
I'm in a cosmic rocket
Racing through the stars.
I think I see Mars,
Oh no! it's just a star,
Lots and lots of stars
Racing past the rocket.
I think I see Mars
Oh yes! it is Mars.
We have now landed
Out we come
And here we go.
What is this?
It looks like slime.
It's oozing out of that pipe.
Who are these blue men
On a red planet?
Here they come.
What is that?
Two heads, four arms
But no legs!
They seem to be friendly
But what is that?
A giant cauldron.
Here they come,
And here we go,
10, 9, 8, 7, 6, 5, 4, 3, 2, 1, blast-off!
Phew we're back on Earth.
I'm never going to Mars again.

Michael Hancock (10)
Winklebury Junior School

THE SLUSHY PLANET

When I was little, I dreamt of a slushy planet,
Made from chocolate milkshake, I try to starve,
But the thought just wouldn't go away.
Shoo! Boom! What was that? A comet?
I decided to go out from here and never come back again.
Soon I was there,
The blushy colour on that planet, a reddy colour,
the red fleshy crest,
Oh! I could just eat it up.
The door behind me slammed, *crash! Bash!*
My heart beats hard.
Ca boom! Ca boom! Ca boom!
I hear a noise, not just any noise, but an unusual noise.
Perhaps it's that ice-cream my mother made,
Or that chocolate cake.
There is only one left, maybe it is.
I've been attacked by *aliens.*
I got tangled and dangled by spider webs.
I can't move with a weird, peculiar, unusual,
Creature! Climbing on my head!
A commotion behind me, I scream.
The planet whirls and twirls,
Spins with twins of creatures.
Rattling noises, zooming and booming.
I'm sinking fast, *someone help me!*
Ahhhhh! Brumm!
I'm back home, oh, I forgot my milkshake.
I am back there,
No!
Why did I say that? *Swoosh!*

Sanda Maung (10)
Winklebury Junior School

PLANET GLOSH

5-4-3-2-1, *blast-off!*
Here we go!
It's really scary *whoosh!*
We are nearly there!
I see the land is bare.
When we arrive on planet Glosh,
We get out and it feels like slosh.
Planet Glosh looks very colourful.
I see something very powerful.
I think there's something with an ugly face.
I see a moon up in space.
I will have my tea.
I've lost my key.
It's getting dark,
But my dog won't bark.
I hear a bang,
And a clang.
There was no alien that was bad,
So I was feeling a bit sad.
I have finished on this planet.
I have to go - *dammit!*

Emily Hull (10)
Winklebury Junior School

A TRIP TO SPACE

I am in bed wishing the day will come for me to have
a trip to space.
As something green splatters on my face
I scream out loud.
I wish I was above the clouds!
As the green mysterious thing comes away,
Then I scream *'It's an alien?'*
Then my mum says 'And it's an ugly one.'

I'm relieved the day has come for me to go into space.
Time for lift-off 5, 4, 3, *'Stop'!*
I forgot my food
Right let's try again 5, 4, 3, 2, 1, *blast-off!*
In space
In space it is a pale pink I think.
Bye bye Milky Way.
Space is a nice place to be.

Kayleigh Peacock (10)
Winklebury Junior School

DESSERTS OF THE MOON

The moon is like semolina in dark brown whip,
Being swallowed up by the black hole.
It's like vanilla ice-cream
On top of raspberry ice-cream
Being dished out by a god above.

The moon is like the spoon
You eat sundae with,
Spinning round a melting pudding
Called Earth!
It feels like cream on chocolate mousse,
Lighting up the little boy's tummy.

It sounds like the bubbling noise
Of bubbles on toffee apples,
As it melts to vanilla milkshake.
It slowly moves from one end of the table
To another,
As it is slowly being cut into pieces,
It's like a soft, smooth banana,
Smothered in chocolate cream.
For it's the moon!

Kerry Taplin
Winklebury Junior School

1, 2, 3, LIFT-OFF!

1, 2, 3, lift-off! Boom! Crackle! Pop!
Up, up in the air blowing my hair.
Boom, crackle, pop!
I'm landing on the moon.
The sun shines with light,
In fact it looks rather bright.
Boom, crackle, pop!
I look down at the earth,
I think it looks tiny
And yet it looks whiney.
Boom, crackle, pop!
Jupiter looks like an orange
with Pluto's lime colour.
It makes me cry and the sun gives a sigh.
Boom, crackle, pop!
Oh look a super flying book.
Boom, crackle, pop!
It's the book of cool rule.
Boom, crackle, pop!
Time to plug the rocket in.
1, 2, 3, lift-off!
Boom, crackle, pop!
Whooooh and wheeeeeee!
Boom, crackle, pop!
Landed on earth.
Mission completed.

Jemma Hilden (10)
Winklebury Junior School

THE ALIEN ON MARS

Zoom, boom - help where am I?
I'm in space.
I've lost my place.
Oh! what am I going to do?
I see a spaceship.
I'm amazed.
I look in it - it's like a maze,
To my surprise.
Oh! What can I see - a lovely green creature!
It looks like a bee,
I go over to see,
To see what was the matter.
I hear a squelch
And a belch.
Oh! Pardon you.
Oh! Good heavens.
It's an *Alien.*
He goes over to the ship.
I looked at the moon,
It thought I was doomed.
Bad luck - you're doomed.
Hey! What do you mean?
What are you doing?
I'm going back to plant *Ziz a zig*
Ahhhhh!

Lisa Thomas (10)
Winklebury Junior School

ALIENS

The aliens are coming what shall I do,
They're getting closer,
They have landed.
They are coming to get us,
Run for your lives to get away.
Hide in the bushes, they will never find us here.
It is getting very dark,
The aliens are gleaming light in the mysterious world.
I would not let him around for tea,
Look the aliens, they're coming for us,
Just run away they will never get us.
Just keep on running, we will soon get away,
If we don't we will be their tea,
Just run we will loose them soon.
At last we lost them, now we can go home.

Ben Blackman (9)
Winklebury Junior School

THE PLANET MARS

One time I went to a planet Mars.
I sprang out to see Mars, I loved it.
They did not have vegetable soup.
They had Mars soup, at last I finished.
It was cool and cold.
It was like magic come true.
As it came dark I saw the stars and the moon too.
The sound went down.
The spaceship went down for the night.
I went 10, 9, 8, 7, 6, 5, 4, 3, 2, 1.
I was floating asleep and that was the end of me.

Sian Hawkins (9)
Winklebury Junior School

THE PLANETS IN ORBIT

5-4-3-2-1- blast-off!
There goes the rocket looking at all the different planets.
Sparkling stars and the Milky Way.
Aliens jumping on the planet Mars.
Rumbling planets green and red.
The gleaming sun,
Hot and bright in the sky.
Suddenly there is a crash.
Oh my! The rocket has crashed on Mars.
Aliens start jumping about.
The rocket's moving up and down.
Starts tumbling down.
Everyone's shouting.
The aliens are still jumping about.
Spacemen praying to stop this thing.
The aliens stop jumping about.
Suddenly there is a mighty explosion.
Everyone abandons the rocket.
We are about to be saved.
There is a rocket.
But hang-on, isn't this the alien's ship?
I wonder if there is another rocket in sight.
I don't think my crew fancy being this alien's tea.

Melanie Roberts (10)
Winklebury Junior School

PLANET OF THE DINGDONGS

10, 9, 8, 7, 6, 5, 4, 3, 2, 1 . . . *Lift off!*
We're off at last! Shooting past
New York city - it's a pity,
We can't stay!
Twisting and turning, I wonder if space,
Is my place.
Look the moon! Does this mean doom?
This is peculiar, what planet is this?
Wow! Look over there
How come, there's a bear!
No, not a bear - a dingdong!
This planet is called Dingdong.
And it really does pong,
This planet is magical, pretty but puzzling.
Oh no! The dingdongs are starting to sing!
Let's go home, I don't like this planet,
Or the dingdongs' song,
'OK' says the captain,
'But I like the dingdongs and the planet's pong!'
Whoosh! We're flying past,
Shooting stars that last,
Forever! Planet Dingdong is nice,
But space,
Is definitely not my place!

Susanna Kempinski (10)
Winklebury Junior School

THE UNKNOWN PLANET

Zoom! Boom! Sonic boom,
Hovercrafts are hovering above your chair - where?
Where! I don't care - they're hovering in your hair!
Have they got *X-ray* vision?
This is mad, this is queer, this is in your ear!
This is odd, this is weird and unknown.
Look there's witchcraft - she's not very nice.
What's coming out of her nails, it's yellow and gooey?
I'm on an unknown planet - I don't know what to do!
What is that line in the air - I stop and stare!
Bleep-bleep-bleep-bleep blop-blop-blop
ding-ding-ding clock-clock-clock.
Is this an *alien code?* I hope not.
They might be bleeping and blopping and dinging and
clocking about me!
My spaceshuttle is on the other side of this planet.
I walk, I come to a road - this is space - not the world.
But all of the cars look like cars - but they are not cars.
This planet, what's it's name? it hasn't got a name.
Have these *aliens* discovered electricity?
They might have, it is all one big question!
I don't know, this planet has got 10 suns,
while we only have one.
Since I am the first person on this planet.
Maybe they will name it after me.
Dilly David or silly David - that should do the trick!

David Goswell (10)
Winklebury Junior School

THE TWO COMETS

A glistening, whistling comet
Shooting across the sky.
I stand and watch while this
Ball of rock and sizzling dust
Crosses us - as it goes by!

This dark dull night, so black
And deadly, the only thing that
Lights up the sky,
Is the glowing moon and
The glittering shiny
Comet!

I saw a different bright
Light, it was practically
The same as the comet.
I wondered what could
It be? It was whistling
Across the sky, I knew
What it was, it was
A comet!

It was very unusual, but
The two comets got closer together
And suddenly all you heard
was *bang!*
The two beautiful glistening
Comets - *collided!*

Leanne Henstock (11)
Winklebury Junior School

ALIEN COMET

Dark, scary, cold, hazy,
Tonight no stars - they're being lazy,
At least the moon is out tonight
Even though it's not very bright.

The crystal stars suddenly appeared,
That star over there - looks extremely weird!
It doesn't look weird because it looks like it has a beard,
It's moving very fast,
But stars don't move!
I think it's coming down, down, down,
Crash, bang! It's hit the ground!

I slowly walked to where
I heard it land.
I stood still and stared
It was a giant black ball of dust and rock.
It wasn't a star from afar,
A giant ball of dust and rock
A round burning comet!

Not just a comet,
There's something green on it!
A small green egg,
Oh no! It's hatching!
Out came its head - then a leg,
It's an orange-eyed, green furry alien!
Now I see an arm,
Don't scream! I must stay calm!

Ruth Adans (11)
Winklebury Junior School

TO SPACE AND BACK

I am going to space;
I will go to Mars,
Jupiter and the Milky Way.

I am in Mars
There are no cars on the motorway.
I am on the way to Jupiter,
There are green aliens,
I say 'Hello' there is no answer.
It goes dark and I get scared,
I scream and shout and run about.

I say Milky Way
Is where we will stay,
I count from ten down to one
I suck my thumb,
All of a sudden I hear.
'Danny it's dinner time.'
And that is the end of the space ride.

Sarah Bartlett (10)
Winklebury Junior School

THE SUN

The sun is a football,
Mixed with different colours.
It is a lion's head.
It is a burning ball of fire.
It is an egg,
Sizzling in a frying pan,
Spitting out balls of fire.
Swirling, slowly,
Like a Frisbee - about to land!

Paula Thomson (9)
Winklebury Junior School

THE PLANET HICCUP

As I soared through space,
The rockets blowing in my face,
Then with a loud *bang!*
I came from space.
Down, down I went,
Then I stumbled on a rather strange place
With a rather rocky land.
As I went round, round and round,
I suddenly realised this was no ordinary place,
As there was a loud *bang!*
Then a big, big hole appeared,
And I met a rather strange creature.
His name was Hiccup.
Then he made a loud *bang!*
Then all goo came out of him,
Flowing, flowing all on the land.
So I got into my little spaceship and flew away,
Calling the planet Hiccup planet.

Michael Large (10)
Winklebury Junior School

THE MOON

The moon is the colour of a dolphin,
It growls like a gigantic bear,
It's shaped like a bouncy beach ball,
Whirling, twirling wherever it can,
A football plunging through the air,
Dancing round and round like an elephant,
Changing its shape and size,
Like a pale white face with a background of black hair,
And as cold as a freezer at home.

Sarah Lilly (11)
Winklebury Junior School

THE PLANET CHOCO

The planet Choco is near the Milky Way.
Some Choco aliens are on the loose.
Little cars go broom, broom, broom all night.
I'm sure it's people from earth.
They eat something in a bun,
They see me, they start to run,
And then start to shout for help.
They get into a rocket.
They play on a bar.
The powerful wind blows them up and down.
They are so quiet you think they are not there.
No, there is no one there.

Michael Spiers (9)
Winklebury Junior School

THE MOON

The moon is a rusk biscuit,
Without any colour.

It moves slowly and stiffly in the air,
And appears from nowhere.

Its shape is like a doughnut,
Without the hole.

When you touch it,
It falls like white dust in your hands.

It sounds like a fizzy drink,
Sizzling up.

It is so white,
Like a snowy polar bear.

Charlene Howard (11)
Winklebury Junior School

THE BLACK HOLE

The black hole is like a big vacuum
in outer space.
Meteors crashing down
in big balls of fire.
Crash! A - UFO!

The *alien* is tall like Michael Jordan
He has size 11 shoes
He has blue glimmering eyes
and red and yellow hair.
He has 10 gigantic fingers
ten enormous toes
two sticky tongues.
He has a brass chest
that can suck things in . . .

Major Mark Ojar (8)
Winklebury Junior School

ON THE MOON

I was scared - I was shivering,
Something was coming towards me,
I started floating in the air,
My sandwich came with me,
I felt sick as I was floating,
I felt like I was hopeless,
It was misty in the air,
The signpost said *beware!*
I got into my rocket,
10, 9, 8, 7, 6, 5, 4, 3, 2, 1.
Zoom!
It felt good to be at home.

Kirsty Hendle (9)
Winklebury Junior School

BUTTERFLY PLANET

I see planet *butterfly*
as I eat a great big pie.
I wonder, I wonder how cool it would be to fly.
Boom, boom, zoom across the air.
I wish I could be a *butterfly* planet
and see the *butterfly* aliens.
They say *'Take us with you'*
I bite my nail,
As I turn all pale.
Oh! They're gone.
I wonder where from.
I bet they're bad,
I would write it on my pad.
There are strange places
And weird little faces.
I could see the whole galaxy
Speaking of galaxy
I wish I had one to eat.
5-4-3-2-1 *zero*
Now I'm a hero.
Go and fly
And don't forget to say *bye-bye!*

Jamie Bugden (9)
Winklebury Junior School

THE ALIEN

I go up in my spaceship
I land on Mars.
I get out of my spaceship
I look around the planet
All I see is a black hole!

I fall for miles but I hit a great big spaceship
I got into the spaceship.
As I was about to go
A great big *alien* grabbed me.
He knocked me out and he pulled me into
a great big cave but I woke up.
I saw an *alien* with 4 eyes, 4 hairy arms
and he had 5 hairy legs.
He was very ugly - he pulled his laser gun out on me
The *alien* let me go and get into the spaceship.
I was taking off.
When I got to Earth the *alien* was in the spaceship.
I got out of the spaceship and the *alien* was behind me.
Everyone was scared and they ran away because they saw him.
I took the *alien* back to Mars and I went back to Earth!

Kenny Lewis (10)
Winklebury Junior School

A SOUNDLESS PLANET

A soundless planet - it gave me a fright.
I saw the soundless planet - it burned my skin.
I tried to get off the soundless planet
A bit of the planet went into my mouth.
It tastes sour!
It is a round planet and I never return.

David Dunn (11)
Winklebury Junior School

UP, UP, AND AWAY

Up, up and away,
Yes, we're going to space today.
Up, up, into the sky,
I know let's play - I spy.

It's very bright in this spot,
Cor! I can spy a lot.
Look I can see the sun,
This is great fun.

Twisting, turning, everywhere,
Those stars make out a pretty bear!
Look at that alien trying to look fashionable,
But he just looks silly and casual.

Up, up, and away,
Yes, we're going to space today.
Up, up, into the sky,
I know, let's play - I spy.

Ceri Joslin (11)
Winklebury Junior School

SHOOTING STARS

Shooting rocket,
In the wonderful black twinkling stars in the sky.
Silver spoon in the sky with the moon.
Flying slow in the dark, cold night.
Teeth chattering in the dark, damp sky.
Crystals like snowflakes dropping from the sky.

Annabelle Gray (11)
Winklebury Junior School

MARS

Bright red cherry,
not being picked.
Bright red football,
not being played with.
Its own life,
not been found yet!
Old red saucer,
Sits alone in the loft.
A blob of strawberry jam,
Slopped on a black painted wall.
It's like a rich red apple,
floating in a bowl of water.
A red *danger* sign,
protecting Mars - the god of war!

Catherine Goswell (11)
Winklebury Junior School

ALIEN AT THE BACK OF THE CLASSROOM

I'm a slimy alien
At the back of the classroom
No one knows I'm here
I have big blue eyes
I have bright green eyes
I have curly purple hair
I've got 10 sharp fingers
On my slimy hands
My spaceship's on the roof
I come from Mars!

Lynsey MacDonald (8)
Winklebury Junior School

Landing On The Moon

Landing on the moon,
Such an extreme thing,
Landing on the moon,
With a great thump!
Landing on the moon,
Is very, very hard - but we've made it!
Getting ready in my spacesuit,
Raring to go,
I'm getting out of the spaceship.
It's very, very cold
I turn my head to see . . .
Aaahhh! An alien.
Back in the spaceship,
Off I go at once,
I was not going to stay around,
To see what would happen to me!

Daniel Martin (10)
Winklebury Junior School

Crazy!

The look, the smell,
Space is a lovely place to dwell!
There's no one else up here
To the sun - we're very near.

This is a very nice planet - Earth
Full of lovely, wonderful, turf.
Sometimes we are moany
Because we are lonely!

I want a Toblerone,
or an ice-cream cone,
But you can't get one.
Because in space there is none!

The look, the smell,
Space is a wonderful place to dwell!

Robert Betherton (11)
Winklebury Junior School

COSMIC

I saw some spaceships last night
Or maybe I was dreaming!

I can't tell mum or dad
'Cause they will not believe me!

I wondered who was in it
Perhaps an *alien's* there!

He came into my bedroom
When I was fast asleep

I found him in my cupboard
He had multi-coloured hair.

But now he is my friend
He sleeps inside my drawer.

Mum and dad have never seen him!
I haven't let them yet.

Louise Blow (8)
Winklebury Junior School

ALIEN

Alien, alien - do you want to play?
Because I must go.
I must go at the end of the day.
You might think I'm crazy
But I'm really lazy
Oh, do you want a daisy?
I have one in my pocket along with a locket.
You are a little bit boring
So now I will start snoring.
You have done nothing all day.
So now I must go,
And say *hello!*
To my *bro!*
Down in San Francisco!

Lee Argent (11)
Winklebury Junior School

SATURN

Saturn is a golden marble
moving round and round
as it orbits the sun.

Its ring is like a bottle top
spinning
as it tilts to the right.

Saturn's like an orange
or a saucer
as it spins and never gets dizzy.

Kimberley Green (10)
Winklebury Junior School

WHAT IS THE MOON

The moon is a white plate
floating through the air.
It is a silver ball
gliding across the blackness.
It is a white Frisbee,
thrown too high.
The moon is a child
playing with the stars.
It is a snowflake
drifting down.
It is a white dove
Flying through the air.
It is a flower,
blooming only at night.

Sebastian Long (11)
Winklebury Junior School

ALIENS

Do you believe in *aliens?*
Because if you don't - *I do!*
I found them last night,
I went outside to a farm full of crops
I saw some mysterious crop circles.
It was spooky outside
Without my mum and dad.
That night there were strange noises
Outside our house
Like ghosts coming in
And werewolves howling!

Liam Mitchell (8)
Winklebury Junior School

THE HOLE THROUGH PLUTO

Up in space here comes.

Up a rocket up, up and away
Straight up and twirling and twisting.

Round and round. Oh no! The rocket is not
controlling itself.

The rocket is still twisting, turning around and round
Spinning rapidly.
Rolling about - zooming past the sun.
Oh no! We've crashed into the moon.
Oh no! The rocket went straight through the stars
Went past all the planets and through the moon
We made a hole in the moon with our rocket!

Layla Chamberlain (10)
Winklebury Junior School

COMETS

It's dark - suddenly a sparkle appears,
Brighter, brighter and brighter it glows,
It gets closer and closer
It appears as a comet.
It's the only thing in sight,
On this lonely night.
Then soon a fright!
It really was a terrible sight,
I thought the comet was going to collide
The comet was an amazing fireball
Hurtling through the sky!

Paul Rickman (10)
Winklebury Junior School

ALIEN IN SPACE

I was flying through the air
nobody to be there.

Out pops an *alien*
and gives me a scare.

It crawled up on the rocket
staring at me with his 4 popping eyes.

His face glistening and glittering - in a sly way.
He was stunned to see a human - though he'd never seen one before.

His face was surprised
like you have never seen before!

Jodie Bramhall (11)
Winklebury Junior School

THE MOON

The moon is an old man,
Snoring in bed.
It is a jellyfish,
Floating through the sea.
The moon is a frozen bag of ice cubes
It's a silver ball,
Flying past the night sky.
The moon is a sparkling milk top,
Waiting to be found,
It's a silver coin,
Being tossed into space.

Louise Hendle (10)
Winklebury Junior School

BLACK HOLE

The black hole is like an air vent on a black wall,
continuously inhaling litter and air.

It is a colossal black sponge,
absorbing water, at will,
like a plughole in a black sink,
draining the water,
sucking in stones.

The black hole is a Hoover
that is unstoppable
and more powerful than ever!

Thomas Bacon
Winklebury Junior School

THUNDER AND LIGHTNING

One night the clouds clumped up together
When no one was looking
                    Bang!
The lightning had an argument with the tree
Soon a fight broke out.
                    Bang!
The tree collapsed
The thunder and lightning were winning
The lightning was scaring and the thunder was killing!
The lightning was lighting up the sky like a lamp
The thunder was making the sky black like a
Bag of coal.

Rosa Harrington (9)
Worting Junior School

THE SNOW

The snow is a blanket of fur on the ground.

Silence everywhere.

The snow comes from the sky
falling down on the ground.
The snow is like the white clouds
up in the sky.
It drops on the roofs of the houses and the
doors of the homes.

It lies like white petals.

Allan Woolford (8)
Worting Junior School

THE SNOW

It came in the morning like a white ice-cream.
It settled like fluffy clouds.
It froze then melted into water.
Then it vanished.
But it came back the next day.

David Andrews (9)
Worting Junior School

THE RAIN

The rain is like drops out of a tap
The sea goes *whoosh! Whoosh!*
The rain sounds out
Drip! Drop!

Shaun Fitzpatrick (7)
Worting Junior School

THE SUN

Out of the house the sun lay like an orange football,
But the fog crept silently like a never-ending path
of smoke.
The sun vanished.
The sun frowned
And it came up with a fright.
Bash! Bang! Boom!
The sun won.
The fog scuttled sadly away.

Adam Gary Walters (9)
Worting Junior School

SNOW FALLING

One snowy morning it looked like
there was cotton wool falling
down onto the ground.
Suddenly the clouds came floating down
Every bit of snow came down.
The clouds swayed down like tissue paper.

Zoey Rampton (8)
Worting Junior School

A WET DAY

I saw a puddle - like a great grey ocean.
A river rumbling and raging - through the street.
The puddle ploughs the street - like a plane.
Plenty of puddles in the street - like rivers racing the rain!

Jamie Freemantle (8)
Worting Junior School

THUNDER AND LIGHTNING

A loud *bang* came from the black sky
a sky as black as ink.
Bang went the thunder and lightning
as loud as music and as
bright as light.
Across the world the lightning
flashes
with thunder.

Alvin Cotter (9)
Worting Junior School

THE STORM

The clouds are starting to get grey,
What was that? Oh! I must pray!
Thunder sounds, the cymbals crashing,
It sounds like a safari park!
Lions lashing,
Thank goodness it's dying down,
Oh why am I on the ground?

Aisling Messenger (9)
Worting Junior School

THUNDER

The thunder goes *bang!*
It's louder than someone shouting
The tree is dying
Lightning has struck!

Sam Harris (7)
Worting Junior School

SNOWY DAY

Ice-cream spread across the ground.
More snow came pouring down
Like solid milkshake melting.
It settled like glistening gems,
It felt like white powder,
It looked like an ice cube
Smashed on the ground.

Louise Abbotts (9)
Worting Junior School

A SNOWY MORNING

The snow came down like cotton wool
and landed softly.
It felt like a soft pillow
It looked like sheep's wool.
I went out
I touched it
and it looked as soft as snow.

Matthew Cox (8)
Worting Junior School

SMILING SUN

Happily the sun moves along
Shining as bright as a little lamp
Brightly looking through the clouds
And it's as bright as a yellow daffodil.

Lori-Ann Chapman (8)
Worting Junior School